AQA AS Level Computer Science
2nd Edition

P.M. Heathcote

R.S.U. Heathcote

Published by
PG Online Limited
The Old Coach House
35 Main Road
Tolpuddle
Dorset
DT2 7EW
United Kingdom
sales@pgonline.co.uk
www.pgonline.co.uk
2016

PG ONLINE

Acknowledgements

We are grateful to the AQA Examination Board for permission to use questions from past papers.

The answers in the Teacher's Supplement are the sole responsibility of the authors and have neither been provided nor approved by the examination board.

We would also like to thank the following for permission to reproduce copyright photographs:

Screenshots of Arriva Bus App © Arriva PLC
Colossus photograph © The National Archives
Google Maps 'StreetView' © Google 2015
Other photographic images © Shutterstock

Graphics: Roger Stayte and Rob Heathcote

Cover picture © 'Golden Moor' 2014
Oil on canvas
Reproduced with the kind permission of Heather Duncan
www.heatherduncan.com

Design and artwork by OnThree
www.on-three.com

Typeset by Chapter One (London) Ltd

First edition 2015, reprinted 2016
Second edition 2016, reprinted 2016

Preface

The aim of this textbook is to provide detailed coverage of the topics in the new AQA AS Level Computer Science specification.

The book is divided into six sections and within each section, each chapter covers material that can comfortably be taught in one or two lessons.

In the first year of this course there will be a strong emphasis on learning to program. You will start by learning the syntax of your chosen programming language – that is, the rules of how to write correct statements that the computer can understand. Then you will code simple programs, building up your skills to the point where you can understand and make additions and amendments to a program consisting of several hundred lines of code.

Sections 1 and 2 of this book can be studied in parallel with your practical programming sessions. It will give you practice in the skills you need to master.

At the end of the year, if you are sitting the AS level exam, Paper 1 will test your general knowledge of programming and your ability to code, and ask you to add and make amendments to a substantial program which you will have had a chance to look at and run beforehand.

Paper 2 will test your knowledge and understanding of the theory parts of the specification.

If you are sitting the A level exam after two years, rather than the AS level, these papers will be a useful end-of-year test of your grasp of the subject, before you go on to cover the second half of the specification.

Each chapter contains exercises and questions, some from past examination papers, and answers to all these are available to teachers only in a Teachers Supplement which can be ordered from our website **www.pgonline.co.uk**.

Approval message from AQA

This textbook has been approved by AQA for use with our qualification. This means that we have checked that it broadly covers the specification and we are satisfied with the overall quality. Full details of our approval process can be found on our website.

We approve textbooks because we know how important it is for teachers and students to have the right resources to support their teaching and learning. However, the publisher is ultimately responsible for the editorial control and quality of this book.

Please note that when teaching the AS Level Computer Science course, you must refer to AQA's specification as your definitive source of information. While this book has been written to match the specification, it cannot provide complete coverage of every aspect of the course.

A wide range of other useful resources can be found on the relevant subject pages of our website: www.aqa.org.uk.

Contents

Section 4

Hardware and software   99

Section 5

Computer organisation and architecture   125

Section 6

Communication: technology and consequences   158

Section 1

Fundamentals of programming

In this section:

1

Chapter 1 – Programming basics

Objectives

- Define what is meant by an algorithm and pseudocode
- Learn how and when different data types are used
- Learn the basic arithmetic operations available in a typical programming language
- Become familiar with basic string handling operations
- Distinguish between variables and constants

What is an algorithm?

An algorithm is a set of rules or a sequence of steps specifying how to solve a problem. A recipe for chocolate cake, a knitting pattern for a sweater or a set of directions to get from A to B, are all algorithms of a kind. Each of them has **input**, **processing** and **output**. We will be looking in more detail at properties of algorithms in Section 2 of this book.

Q1: What are the inputs and outputs in a recipe, a knitting pattern and a set of directions?

Ingredients	Method
100g plain flour	Put flour and salt into a large mixing bowl and make a well in the centre.
2 eggs	
300ml milk	Crack the eggs into the middle.
1tbsp oil	Pour in about 50ml milk and the oil.
Pinch salt	Start whisking from the centre, gradually drawing the flour into the eggs, milk and oil, etc.

In the context of programming, the series of steps has to be written in such a way that it can be translated into program code which is then translated into machine code and executed by the computer.

Using pseudocode

Whatever programming language you are using in your practical work, as your programs get more complicated you will need some way of working out what the steps are before you sit down at the computer to type in the program code. A useful tool for developing algorithms is **pseudocode**, which is a sort of halfway house between English and program statements. There are no concrete rules or syntax for how pseudocode has to be written, and there are different ways of writing most statements. We will use a standard way of writing pseudocode that translates easily into a programming language such as Python, Pascal or whatever procedural language you are learning.

This book does not teach you how to program in any particular programming language – you will learn how to write programs in your practical sessions – but it will help you to understand and develop your own algorithms to solve problems.

An introduction to pseudocode statements

Input/output statements

Most programs will have input and output statements to allow the user to enter data and display or print results. Here is the pseudocode for a simple example:

```
OUTPUT "What is your name? "                    #display text on the screen
#wait for user input and assign the value to the variable myname
myname ← USERINPUT
OUTPUT "Hello, ",myname
```

This program will ask the user to input their name, and then display "Hello, Jo" or whatever name the user entered. Notice that in this pseudocode, text such as "Hello," will be wrapped in speech marks to distinguish it from variables.

We will also use the pseudocode

```
myname ← USERINPUT "What is your name? "
```

which combines the OUTPUT and USERINPUT statement to display the prompt "What is your name? " and then wait for the user to enter text and press the ENTER key.

Comments

Note also that anything following a # will be treated as a **comment** and will have no effect on the running of the program. Comments are very important when you come to code your programs, to document the code (specifying the name, author, date written and purpose of the program, for example) and to explain how any tricky bits of the program work.

Data types

All programming languages have built-in elementary data types. Different data types are held differently in the computer's memory so you need to use the correct data type for the task. The most common data types include:

- integer   a whole number such as -25, 0, 3, 28679

- real/float   a number with a fractional part such as -13.5, 0.0, 3.142, 100.0001

- Boolean   a Boolean variable can only take the value TRUE or FALSE

- character   a letter or number or special character typically represented in ASCII, such as a, A, ? or %. Note that the character "4" is represented differently in the computer from the integer 4 or the real number 4.0

- string   anything enclosed in quote marks is a string, for example "Peter", "123", or "This is a string". Either single or double quotes are acceptable in many languages.

Common arithmetic operations

The symbols +, -, * and / are used for the common arithmetic operations of addition, subtraction, multiplication and division.

e.g. Suppose the bill in a restaurant comes to £20, and you want to divide it equally among 3 or 4 friends.

```
bill ← 20
billBetween4 ← bill/4      will return the value 5
billBetween3 ← bill/3      returns 6.666666667
```

1-1

In pseudocode you can assume that `billBetween3` will be automatically defined as a real variable and will store a value such as 6.666666667, though this may not be the case in every programming language.

The Round function

You can round this number using a function `round`.

```
billBetween3 ← round(billBetween3,2)     #round to 2 decimal places
```

This will return the value 6.67.

The Trunc function

Some languages have a truncate or `trunc` function, which rounds a real number down to the nearest whole number.

Q2: How could you convert this answer to a string variable and assign the answer to billstring?

Exponentiation

If you want to find, for example 2^5, 5 is called the **exponent** and you need to use exponentiation. You can write this operation in pseudocode as:

```
x ← 2**5
```

or, using variables as:

```
x ← y**n
```

Integer division and finding a remainder

Sometimes you may want to perform **integer division** and find a **remainder**.

For example: Twenty apples are to be divided between 6 people. How many will each receive, and how many will be left over?

In this case you need to use the `div` operator to find the whole number of apples each person will receive. The `mod` operator will find the remainder.

These two operations are coded differently in different programming languages, but in pseudocode you could write the following statements:

```
apples ← 20
applesPerPerson ← 20 div 3        (written applesPerPerson = 20//3 in Python)
```

This will return 6 in `applesPerPerson`.

```
applesRemaining ← 20 mod 3        (written applesRemaining = 20%3 in Python)
```

This will return 2 in `applesRemaining`.

1-1

String-handling functions

Programming languages have a number of built-in string-handling methods or functions. Some of the common ones in a typical language are:

`len(string)`	Returns the length of a string
`string.substring(index1,index2)`	Returns a portion of `string` inclusive of the characters at each index position
`string.find(str)`	Determines if `str` occurs in a string. Returns index (the position of the first character in the string) if found, and -1 otherwise. In our pseudocode we will assume that string(1) is the first element of the string, though in Python, for example, the first element is string(0)
`ord("a")`	Returns the integer value of a character (97 in this example)
`chr(97)`	Returns the character represented by an integer ("a" in this example)

Q3: What will be output by the following lines of code?

```
x = "Come into the garden, Maud"
y = len(x)
z = x.find("Maud")
OUTPUT "x= ",x
OUTPUT "y= ",y
OUTPUT "z= ",z
```

1-1

To **concatenate** or join two strings, use the + operator.

e.g. "Johnny" + "Bates" = "JohnnyBates"

String conversion operations

`int("1")`	converts the character "1" to the integer 1
`str(123)`	converts the integer 123 into a string "123"
`float("123.456")`	converts the string "123.456" to the real number 123.456
`str(123.456)`	converts the real number 123.456 to the string "123.456"
`date(year,month,day)`	returns a number that you can calculate with

Converting between strings and dates is usually handled by functions built in to string library modules, e.g. strtodate("01/01/2016").

Example:

```
date1 ← strtodate("18/01/2015")
date2 ← strtodate("30/12/2014")
days ← date1 - date2
OUTPUT date1, date2, days
```

This will output

```
2015-01-18 2014-12-30 19
```

Constants and variables

Some programming languages require you to declare all variables and constants before they are used in the program. For example:

```
var totalMark: integer
const VAT = 20.0
```

Variables are **identifiers** (names) given to memory locations whose contents will change during the course of the program; we have seen plenty of examples of these – e.g. in the statement below, the variable `myname` will change according to what the user enters.

```
myname ← USERINPUT
```

You should always try to use meaningful names for variables, rather than x, y and z, as this helps to make the program easy to follow and update when required.

Some programming languages also allow you to define **constants**, whose value never changes while the program is being run. For example, if your program involved calculating the area of a circle, you could define pi at the start of the program as a constant having the value 3.14159. Or, you might hold the company phone number as a constant, declared at the start of the program as

```
const companyPhone = "01453 123456"
```

Advantages of using constants

The advantage of using a constant is that in a long, complex program there is no chance that a programmer will accidentally change its value by using the identifier for a different purpose. It also means that if the value of a constant (e.g. VAT) changes from say 20.0 to 17.5, the programmer does not have to hunt through the program to find all the lines where the value 20.0 has been used.

In addition, using constants makes programming code more readable than using values.

Some languages such as Python do not require or even allow you to define variables or constants – you just use them as and when required in the program.

Exercises

1. A school keeps data about each of its pupils. State the most suitable data type for each of the following data items:

    Pupil's surname

    A single letter indicating whether they are male or female

    The amount owed for school trips

    The number of school trips they have participated in

    Whether or not the pupil is entitled to free school meals   [5]

2. (a) Write pseudocode for a program which asks the user to enter the total bill for a restaurant meal, and the total number of people who had a meal. The program should add 10% to the bill as a tip, and then calculate and display to the nearest penny what each person owes, assuming the bill is evenly split.   [6]

Exercises continued

(b) Complete the following table showing an additional **two** sets of test data, the reason for each test and the expected result. [6]

Total bill	Number of people	Reason for test	Expected result
100.00	10	Total amount exactly divisible by number of people	11.00

3. (a) Name **two** ways in which you can help to make your programs understandable for another programmer. [2]

(b) Imagine that you have had a stall at the Summer Fayre. At the end of the day you count up the number of each 1p, 2p, 5p, 10p, 20p and 50p coins you have received.

Write a pseudocode algorithm to allow the user to input the number of coins of each value, and to calculate and display the total takings.

Make use of **two** ways of making the program understandable given in your answer to part (a). [6]

1-1

Chapter 2 – Selection

Objectives

- be able to use relational operators
- be able to use Boolean operations AND, OR, NOT, XOR
- be able to use nested selection statements

Program constructs

There are just three basic programming constructs: **sequence**, **selection** and **iteration**.

Sequence is just two or more statements following one after the other, such as

```
OUTPUT "Please enter a number: "
n ← USERINPUT
nsquared ← n * n
```

The last statement is an **assignment** statement in which a value is **assigned** to a variable.

In this chapter and the next, we will look at selection and iteration.

Selection

Selection statements are used to select which statement will be executed next, depending on some condition. Conditions are formulated using **relational operators**.

Relational operators

The following operators may be used in pseudocode for making comparisons:

- > greater than
- < less than
- >= greater than or equal
- <= less than or equal
- = equal
- <> not equal

Q1: Are these operators the same as the ones used in the programming language you are learning? If not, how are they different?

Selection statements can take different forms, for example:

```
IF (expression1) THEN
    (do these statements)
ENDIF
```

Expression1 is an expression involving a relational operator such as

```
IF (AGE >=17) THEN
    canDrive ← TRUE
ENDIF
```

> **Q2:** What type of variable is `canDrive`?

If `expression1` does not evaluate to TRUE, control passes to the next statement after the IF statement.

Alternatively, you can specify what should happen if the condition does not evaluate to TRUE:

```
IF (expression1) THEN
    (do these statements)
ELSE
    (do these statements)
ENDIF
```

For example:

```
IF mark >= 50 THEN
    OUTPUT "Pass"
ELSE
    OUTPUT "Fail"
    OUTPUT "You will have to retake this test."
ENDIF
```

A 'nested' selection statement may have another IF statement inside one or both of the code blocks for the cases of the outer IF :

```
IF (expression1) THEN
    IF (expression2) THEN
        (do these statements)
    ELSE
        (do these statements)
    ENDIF
ELSE
    (do these statements)
ENDIF
```

Example 1

A bank offers different interest rates according to how much is in the account. There are three thresholds of £500, £3,000 and £10,000:

If amount less than 500, rate = 1%

If amount greater than or equal £500 but less than £3000, rate = 1.5%

If amount greater than or equal £3000 but less than £10000, rate = 2%

If amount greater than or equal £10000, rate is 3.5%

The selection statement can be written as follows:

```
IF (amount < 500) THEN
    rate ← 0.01
ELSE IF (amount < 3000) THEN
    rate ← 0.015
ELSE IF (amount < 10000) THEN
    rate ← 0.02
ELSE
    rate ← 0.035
ENDIF
```

The CASE statement

Some programming languages support the use of a CASE statement, an alternative structure to a nested IF statement. It is useful when a choice has to be made between several alternatives.

Example 2

Perform different statements according to an option choice entered by the user.

```
CASE choice of
   1: OUTPUT "You have selected option 1"
      (more statements here)
   2: OUTPUT "You have selected option 2"
      (more statements here)
   3: OUTPUT "You have selected option 3"
      (more statements here)
ELSE
   OUTPUT "You must enter 1, 2 or 3"
ENDCASE
```

Example 3

A statement to calculate the number of days in each month between 2001 and 2099 may be written:

```
CASE month of
   "Jan","Mar","May","Jul","Aug","Oct","Dec": daysInMonth ← 31
   "Apr","Jun","Sep","Nov":                   daysInMonth ← 30
   "Feb":  IF year MOD 4 = 0 THEN
               daysInMonth ← 29
           ELSE
               daysInMonth ← 28
           ENDIF
ENDCASE
```

Boolean operators AND, OR, NOT

More complex conditions can be formed using the Boolean operators AND and OR.

Example 4

```
IF (a > b) AND (a > c) THEN
   max ← a
ELSE IF (b > a) AND (b > c) THEN
   max ← b
ELSE
   max ← c
ENDIF
```

Example 5

Write pseudocode for a program to allow the user to input the day of the week and output "Weekday" or "Weekend".

```
day ← USERINPUT
IF (day = "Saturday") OR (day = "Sunday") THEN
   OUTPUT "Weekend"
ELSE
   OUTPUT "Weekday"
ENDIF
```

Example 6

A tourist attraction has a daily charge for children of £5.00 on a weekday, or £7.50 on a weekend or bank holiday. Adults are charged £8.00 on weekdays and £12.00 on weekends and bank holidays. Write pseudocode to allow the user to calculate the charge for a visitor.

```
OUTPUT "Enter W for weekend, B for bank holiday or D for weekday"
day ← USERINPUT
OUTPUT "Enter A for adult, C for child"
visitor ← USERINPUT
IF ((day = "W") OR (day = "B")) AND (visitor = "A") THEN
   charge ← 12.0
ELSE IF ((day = "W") OR (day = "B")) AND (visitor = "C") THEN
   charge ← 7.5
ELSE IF (visitor = "A") THEN
   charge ← 8.0
ELSE
   charge ← 5.0
ENDIF
```

1-2

Notes:

It is important to use brackets and to get them in the correct place to avoid any confusion over which operator is processed first. In standard Boolean logic the precedence rules make NOT highest, then AND, then OR.

The NOT operator

You can usually avoid the use of the NOT operator, replacing it with an appropriate condition.
e.g.

```
NOT (a = b)  is equivalent to  a <> b
NOT (a < b)  is equivalent to  a >= b
```

The XOR operator

XOR stands for **exclusive OR**, so that a XOR b means "either a or b but not both".

This can be implemented with a combination of AND, OR and NOT conditions:

```
(a AND NOT b) OR (NOT a AND b)
```

Note that NOT takes precedence over AND. Add extra brackets if you are in any doubt!

Exercises

1. Below is a segment of an algorithm to determine at what times different members are allowed to use the competition pool at the local Sports Centre.

```
swimTime ← False
IF (Membership = "Premier") THEN
    swimTime ← TRUE
ELSE IF ((Membership = "Adult") AND (Day = "Weekday") AND
        (Time < 1500)) OR
        ((Membership = "Adult") AND (Day = "Weekend")) THEN
    swimTime ← TRUE
ELSE IF (Membership = "Junior") AND (Day = "Weekend") THEN
    swimTime ← TRUE
ENDIF
```

Write down the values of swimTime after the segment of the algorithm has executed with the following data:

(i)   Membership: Premier   Day: Weekday   Time: 1700

(ii) Membership: Adult   Day: Weekday   Time: 1100

(iii) Membership: Junior   Day: Weekday   Time: 1000

(iv) Membership: Adult   Day: Weekend   Time: 0900

(v)   Membership: Adult   Day: Weekday   Time: 1530   [5]

2. (a) Write a pseudocode algorithm for a program which calculates the cost of carpeting a room. The carpet is supplied in a roll 4m wide. The cost of the carpet is £10 per square metre. The program should ask the user to enter the longest dimension (length) and shortest dimension (width) of the room, then calculate and display the length and width and cost of carpet that will be supplied.

   You can assume that the width of the room is not more than 4m. If a width of more than 4m is entered, display an error message and quit the program.

   The length could be more or less than 4m.   [5]

   (b) Calculate the expected results for the following room sizes:

   Length = 5,   width = 3

   Length = 5,   width = 4

   Length = 3,   width = 2

   Length = 3.9, width = 2

   Length = 6,   width = 5   [5]

Chapter 3 – Iteration

Objectives

- Understand and use three different types of iterative statement WHILE, REPEAT and FOR
- Be familiar with, and be able to use, random number generation

Performing a loop

In the last two chapters we looked at **sequence** and **selection** statements. The third programming construct is **iteration**. Iteration means repetition, so iterative statements always involve performing a loop in the program to repeat a number of statements. There are three different types of loop to be considered, although some programming languages do not implement all three.

- **Indefinite iteration** where the iteration continues until some specified condition is met, includes WHILE … ENDWHILE loops and REPEAT … UNTIL loops
- **Definite iteration**, where the number of times the loop is to be executed is decided in advance, is implemented using FOR … ENDFOR loop

The WHILE … ENDWHILE loop

A WHILE … ENDWHILE loop has two properties:

- The expression controlling the repetition of the loop must be of type Boolean – that is, one which evaluates to True or False
- This expression is tested at the **start** of the loop

1-3

This is best explained by means of an example. Suppose you wanted to input the daily maximum temperatures for one month, calculate and output the average of these measurements.

The program has to work for any month, so when you have entered all the temperatures you will enter a 'dummy' value -100 to signify that there are no more temperatures to enter.

A first attempt at the pseudocode might look like this:

```
temp ← 0                  #initialise temp
totalTemp ← 0             #initialise total of temperatures
numberOfTemps ← 0         #initialise number of temperatures
WHILE temp <> -100
   OUTPUT "Enter next temperature"
   temp ← USERINPUT
   totalTemp ← totalTemp + temp
   numberOfTemps ← numberOfTemps + 1
ENDWHILE
averageTemp ← totalTemp/numberOfTemps
OUTPUT averageTemp
```

Test this algorithm with temperatures 8, 12 and -100. We can draw a trace table showing the value of the variables as they change during execution of the program.

totalTemp	numberOfTemps	Temp <> -100	temp	averageTemp
0	0	TRUE	8	
8	1	TRUE	12	
20	2	TRUE		

Q1: Complete the trace table. What is the average temperature calculated by this algorithm?

You should have ended up with 3 temperatures and an average temperature of -26.66667 instead of 10. The problem is that the expression controlling the loop is tested only once each time round, at the beginning of the loop, and not after each statement within the loop as it is executed. Therefore, we have to make sure that as soon as the number -100 is entered, the next thing that happens is that the Boolean expression is tested.

```
totalTemp ← 0                 #initialise total of temperatures
numberOfTemps ← 0             #initialise number of temperatures
OUTPUT "Enter next temperature"
temp ← USERINPUT              #input first temperature
WHILE temp <> -100
    totalTemp ← totalTemp + temp
    numberOfTemps ← numberOfTemps + 1
    OUTPUT "Enter next temperature"
    temp ← USERINPUT
ENDWHILE
averageTemp ← totalTemp/numberOfTemps
OUTPUT averageTemp
```

Note that with a WHILE ... ENDWHILE loop, if the Boolean expression is TRUE at the start, the loop will not be executed at all and control will pass straight to the next statement after ENDWHILE.

Q2: What will happen if the first temperature entered is -100? Alter the algorithm to ensure that the program displays a suitable message.

The REPEAT ... UNTIL loop

This type of loop is very similar to the WHILE ... ENDWHILE loop, with the difference that the Boolean expression controlling the loop is written and tested at the end of the loop, rather than at the beginning. This means that the loop is always performed at least once.

Note:

Python does not support a REPEAT ... UNTIL statement, but the same output can be achieved with a WHILE ... ENDWHILE loop.

1-3

Example 1

Write pseudocode for a program which tests someone on the squares of numbers up to 25.

```
#program to test a user on the squares of numbers
#random(a,b) generates a random integer between a and b

REPEAT
   num ← random(1,25)
   numsquare ← num * num
   OUTPUT "What is the square of ", num
   answer ← USERINPUT()
   IF answer = numsquare THEN
      OUTPUT "Correct, well done"
   ELSE
      OUTPUT "No, it is ", numsquare
   ENDIF
   OUTPUT "Another go? Answer Y or N"
   anotherGo ← USERINPUT
UNTIL (anotherGo = "N") OR (anotherGo = "n")
```

Q3: Rewrite this algorithm using a WHILE ... ENDWHILE loop. Which loop do you think is preferable for performing this task?

The FOR ... ENDFOR loop

This type of loop is useful when you know how many iterations need to be performed. For example, suppose you want to display the two times table:

```
FOR count ← 1 TO 12
   product ← 2 * count
   OUTPUT "2 x ", count, " = ", product
ENDFOR
```

The value of count starts at 1 and is incremented each time round the loop. When it reaches 12, the loop terminates and the next statement is executed.

Nested loops

Loops can be "nested" one inside another. Suppose we want to display all the multiplication tables between 1 and 12. We can do this with two FOR loops, one inside the other.

Example 2

```
FOR table ← 1 TO 12
   FOR count ← 1 TO 12
      product ← table * count
      OUTPUT table, " x ", count, " = ", product
   ENDFOR
ENDFOR
```

Q4: What will be the second line output by this algorithm?

Example 3

Use a random number generator to simulate throwing a die to find out how many throws it takes to get a 6.

```
answer ← "y"
WHILE (answer = "y") or (answer = "Y")
   numberOfThrows ← 0
   throw ← 0
   WHILE throw <> 6
      throw ← random(1,6)
      numberOfThrows ← numberOfThrows + 1
      OUTPUT "You threw a ", throw
   ENDWHILE
   OUTPUT "That took ",numberOfThrows," throws"
   OUTPUT "Another go? (Y or y)"
   answer ← USERINPUT
ENDWHILE
```

Q5: What will happen if the user answers "yes" in answer to the question "Another go? (Y or y)"?

1-3

Example 4

You can count backwards as well as forwards in a FOR ... ENDFOR loop. Here is a pseudocode program which uses the 'sleep' method to count down in seconds to blast-off. It uses a function called `sleep` which suspends execution for a given number of seconds:

```
ReadyForCountdown ← USERINPUT "Press enter when you're ready to start"
FOR secs ← 10 TO 0 STEP -1
   OUTPUT secs
   sleep(1)              #suspends execution for 1 second
ENDFOR
OUTPUT "BLAST-OFF!"
```

Exercises

1. Write a pseudocode algorithm to allow the user to input two integers **highestNumber** and **multiplier**. The program should output the results of multiplying integers **2, 3... highestNumber** by **multiplier**.

    For example if the user enters 100 for **highestNumber** and 7 for **multiplier** the program should output the numbers 14, 21 ... 700. [5]

2. Write pseudocode for a program that asks the user which times table they would like to be tested on, and then gives them 5 random questions on this table. The computer should tell them each time whether they got the answer right or wrong. [5]

Chapter 4 – Arrays

Objectives

- Be familiar with the concept of a data structure
- Use 1- and 2-dimensional arrays in the design of solutions to simple problems

Data structures

A data structure is a collection of **elementary data types** such as **integer**, **real**, **Boolean**, **char**, and built-in methods to facilitate processing in some way. Computer languages such as Python, Pascal and VB have some built-in **structured data types** such as **string**, **array** or **list** and **record**. Other data structures such as stacks and trees can be created by the programmer to suit a specific purpose.

1-dimensional arrays

An array is defined as a finite, ordered set of elements of the same type, such as integer, real or char. **Finite** means that there is a specific number of elements in the array. **Ordered** implies that there is a first, second, third etc. element of the array.

For example, (assuming the first element of the array is `myArray[0]` and not `myArray[1]`):

```
myArray ← [51, 72, 35, 37, 0, 3]
x ← myArray[2]          #assigns 35 to x
```

Example

Every year the RSPB organises a Big Garden Birdwatch to involve the public in counting the number of birds of different types that they see in their gardens on a particular weekend. During 24-25 January 2015, more than 6 million birds were counted and reported.

The scientists add all the sightings together to find out how birds and other wildlife are doing.

Once this has been checked and pieced together, they can monitor trends and understand how different birds and other wildlife are faring.

An array of strings could be used to hold the names of the birds, and an array of integers to hold the results as they come in. As a simple example we will hold the names of 8 birds in an array:

```
birdName ← ["robin", "blackbird", "pigeon", "magpie", "bluetit",
"thrush", "wren", "starling"]
```

We can reference each element of the array using an **index**. For example:

```
birdName[2] ← "pigeon"  #the index here is 2
```

Most languages have a function which will return the length of an array, so that

```
numSpecies ← len(birdName)
```

will assign 8 to `numSpecies`.

1-4

To find at which position of the array a particular bird is, we could use the following algorithm:

```
bird ← USERINPUT
birdFound ← FALSE
numSpecies ← len(birdName)
FOR count ← 0 TO numSpecies - 1
   IF bird = birdName[count] THEN
      birdIndex ← count
      birdFound ← TRUE
   ENDIF
ENDFOR
IF birdFound = FALSE THEN
   OUTPUT "Bird species not in array"
ELSE
   OUTPUT "Bird found at", birdIndex
ENDIF
```

We need a second array of integers to accumulate the totals of each bird species observed. We can initialise each element to zero.

```
birdCount ← [0,0,0,0,0,0,0,0]
```

To add 5 to the blackbird count (the second element in the list) we can write a statement

```
birdCount[1] ← birdCount[1] + 5
```

The following algorithm enables a member of the Birdwatch team to enter results as they come in from members of the public.

```
birdName ← ["robin", "blackbird", "pigeon", "magpie", "bluetit",
            "thrush", "wren", "starling"]
birdCount ← [0,0,0,0,0,0,0,0]
OUTPUT "Please input name of bird (x to end): "
bird ← USERINPUT
WHILE bird <> "x"
      birdFound ← FALSE
      FOR count ← 0 TO 7
            IF bird = birdName[count] THEN
               birdFound ← TRUE
               OUTPUT "number observed: "
               birdsObserved ← USERINPUT
               birdCount[count] ← birdCount[count] + birdsObserved
            ENDIF
      ENDFOR
      IF birdFound = FALSE THEN
         OUTPUT "Bird species not in array"
      ENDIF
      OUTPUT "Please input name of bird (x to end): "
      bird ← USERINPUT
ENDWHILE
#now print out the totals for each bird
FOR count ← 0 TO 7
      OUTPUT birdName[count], birdCount[count]
ENDFOR
```

1-4

2-dimensional arrays

An array can have two or more dimensions. A two-dimensional array can be visualised as a table, rather like a spreadsheet.

Imagine a 2-dimensional array called `numbers`, with 3 rows and 4 columns. Elements in the array can be referred to by their row and column number, so that `numbers[1][3] = 8` in the example below.

An alternative syntax used in some programming languages is `numbers[1,3]` or `numbers(1,3)`.

	Column 0	**Column 1**	**Column 2**	**Column 3**
Row 0	1	2	3	4
Row 1	5	6	7	8
Row 2	9	10	11	12

Q1: What is the value of `numbers[2][1]`?

Example

Write a pseudocode algorithm for a module which prints out the quarterly sales figures (given in integers) for each of 3 sales staff named Anna, Bob and Carol, together with the total annual sales for all staff. Assume that the sales figures are already in the 2-dimensional array `quarterSales`. The staff names are held in a 1-dimensional array `staff`.

```
staff ← ["Anna","Bob","Carol"]
quarterSales ← [[100,110,120,110],
                [350,355,360,360],
                [200,210,220,220]]
annualSales ← 0
FOR s ← 0 to 2
   #output staff name
   (insert statement here)

   FOR q ← 0 to 3
      OUTPUT "Quarter ",q, quarterSales[s][q]
      annualSales ← annualSales + quarterSales[s][q]
   ENDFOR
ENDFOR
OUTPUT "Annual sales for all staff: ",annualSales
```

Q2: What statement needs to be inserted after the comment `#output staff name` in order to output the staff name?

Arrays of n dimensions

Arrays may have more than two dimensions. An n-dimensional array is a set of elements of the same type, indexed by a tuple of n integers, where a tuple is an ordered list of elements. In a 3-dimensional array x, a particular element may be referred to as `x[4][5][2]`, for example. The first element would be referred to as `x[0][0][0]` (assuming the array indices start at 0 and not 1).

1-4

Exercises

1. Referring to the BirdWatch program given earlier in this chapter:

(a) Explain why the FOR ... ENDFOR loop repeated below is not the most efficient type of loop in this situation. [1]

```
FOR count ← 0 to 7
   IF bird = birdName[count] THEN
      birdFound ← TRUE
      OUTPUT "number observed: "
      birdsObserved ← USERINPUT
      birdCount[count] ← birdCount[count] + birdsObserved
   ENDIF
ENDFOR
```

(b) Rewrite the algorithm using a different type of loop. [3]

2. The birth weights in grams of 100 babies, which vary between 1500 to 4000 grams, are held in an array `weight`.

Write pseudocode for an algorithm which calculates the average birth weight, and then prints out the number of babies who are more than 500 grams below the average weight, together with the average weight of these. [5]

3. The marks for 3 assignments, each marked out of 10, for a class of 5 students are to be input into a two-dimensional array `mark` so that `mark[3][1]`, for example, holds the second mark achieved by the 4th student. Any missing assignments are given a mark of zero.

Draw a table representing this array, and fill it with test data. [2]

Write a pseudocode algorithm which allows the user to enter the marks for the class. Calculate the average mark for each student, and the class average. [4]

4. In a certain game, treasure is hidden in a 10x10 grid. The grid coordinates are given by `grid[row][col]` where `grid[0][0]` represents the top left hand corner and `grid[9][9]` the bottom right corner. The grid coordinates of the treasure are signified by a 1 at `grid[row][col]`. All other grid elements are filled with zeros.

What is the purpose of the following pseudocode algorithm? [2]

```
FOR row ← 0 TO 9
   FOR col ← 0 TO 9
      IF grid[row][col] = 1 THEN
         OUTPUT "row", row, "column", col
      ENDIF
   ENDFOR
ENDFOR
```

Write pseudocode statements to initialise the grid and "hide the treasure" at a random location inside the grid. [5]

Chapter 5 – Subroutines

Objectives

- Be familiar with subroutines, their uses and advantages
- Be able to use subroutines that return values to the calling routine
- Be able to describe the use of parameters to pass data within programs
- Be able to contrast the use of local and global variables

Types of subroutine

A subroutine is a **named block of code** which performs a specific task within a program.

Most high-level languages support two types of subroutine, **functions** and **procedures**, which are called in a slightly different way. Some languages such as Python have only one type of subroutine, namely functions.

All programming languages have 'built-in' functions which you will have already used if you have written any programs. For example, in Python:

```
print("What is your name? ")
myName = input()
print("Hello, ",myName)
age = input("How old are you? ")
```

A subroutine is called by writing its name in a program statement. Some functions return a result, like the `input` function above, and some do not return any result, like the `print` function. Notice that the last statement above combines the **print** and **input** functions; when the statement is executed, the computer will display the question "How old are you?" and wait for the user to input an answer, which will be assigned to the variable `age`.

In languages which distinguish between functions and procedures, a **function** is called like the **input** function above, always assigning a return value to a variable. A **procedure** is called by writing its name but not assigning the result to a variable, like the **print** statement above. However, as we shall see later, a procedure can still pass values back to the calling program if necessary.

In Chapter 1, we listed some string-handling functions, and we can write, for example, pseudocode such as

```
x ← int("567")
```

to call the `int` function, which will convert the string `"567"` into an integer.

> **Q1:** List some other functions you have used in your programs or pseudocode algorithms.
>
> **Q2:** In some languages, `sqrt` is a function which returns the square root of a number. What value will be assigned to the variable `z` by the statement?
>
> ```
> z = sqrt(25)
> ```

User-written subroutines

You can write your own subroutines (functions and/or procedures) and call them from within the program as many times as needed. The subroutine (or subprogram) first needs to be defined, typically above the code in the main program.

Example 1

Using pseudocode, write a subroutine which displays a menu of 4 options in a game.

```
SUB displayMenu                          #declare the subroutine
   OUTPUT "Option 1: Display rules"
   OUTPUT "Option 2: Start new game"
   OUTPUT "Option 3: Quit"
   OUTPUT "Enter 1, 2 or 3: "
ENDSUB
```

To call the subroutine from the main program, you simply write its name:

```
displayMenu
```

This subroutine always produces the same result whenever it is called; it simply displays this menu.

Example 2

Sometimes, you may want a subroutine to return a value to the main program:

```
SUB getChoice
   OUTPUT "Option 1: Display rules"
   OUTPUT "Option 2: Start new game"
   OUTPUT "Option 3: Quit"
   OUTPUT "Enter 1, 2 or 3: "
   choice ← USERINPUT
   RETURN choice
ENDSUB
#main program starts here
option ← getChoice
OUTPUT "You have chosen ", option
```

In this example, when the program is run, the first line to be executed is the first statement in the main program, option ← getChoice. The subroutine is called, it displays the menu, gets the user's choice in choice and returns this to the main program using the statement RETURN choice. Execution continues where it left off, at the statement OUTPUT "You have chosen ", option.

The subroutine is called in a slightly different way from the subroutine displayMenu – compare this to the two different ways in which built-in OUTPUT and USERINPUT subroutines are called.

```
OUTPUT "What is your name?"
myName ← USERINPUT
OUTPUT "Hello, ", myName
```

The OUTPUT subroutine does not return a value, the USERINPUT subroutine does.

Q3: Write pseudocode for a program which

– asks the user "Do you like chocolate?"

– calls a subroutine `getresponse` which ask the user to enter y or n, validates this response and repeats the question until y or n is entered

– prints a suitable comment depending on the answer

Subroutines with interfaces

Frequently, you need to pass values or variables to a subroutine. The exact form of the **subroutine interface** varies with the programming language, but will be similar to the examples below:

```
SUB subroutineName(parameter1, parameter 2,...)
```

There are two mechanisms for passing parameters: by value and by reference. When parameters are passed by value, changing a parameter inside the subroutine will not affect its value outside the subroutine. All parameters are passed this way in Python.

In other languages such as Visual Basic, the programmer can specify whether the parameter is to be passed by value or by reference. When a parameter is passed by reference, the address of the parameter, and not its value, is passed, so any change made to it in a subroutine will be reflected in the calling program.

Example 3

Consider a simple subroutine which calculates the volume of a cylinder. In the main program, the user is asked to enter values for the radius and length of the cylinder. These variables are then passed as **parameters** to the subroutine for use in the calculation.

The values (or addresses) of the parameters `radius` and `length` in line 11 are passed to the subroutine where they are referred to using the identifiers `r` and `len` respectively. The order in which the parameters are written when calling the subroutine is important: `radius` is passed to `r`, `length` is passed to `len`. The return value `vol` is passed back to the main program, where it is assigned to `volume` in line 11.

```
1   SUB cylinderVolume(r,len)
2       pi ← 3.142
3       vol ← pi*r*r*len
4       RETURN vol
5   ENDSUB
6   #main program
7   OUTPUT "Enter the radius of the cylinder:"
8   radius ← USERINPUT
9   OUTPUT "Enter the length of the cylinder:"
10  length ← USERINPUT
11  volume ← cylinderVolume(radius,length)
12  OUTPUT "The volume of the cylinder is ", volume
```

1-5

Q4: Line numbers have been added to each statement of the above pseudocode for reference. Write down the statement numbers in the order in which they are executed.

Q5: Write pseudocode for a program which calls a function `addNumbers(n,m)` to add all the numbers between 5 and 10. The result should be returned to the main program and displayed.

Q6: Write pseudocode for a program which asks the user to enter a name and percentage mark. It then calls a subroutine which assigns a grade to the mark which it passes back to the main program, where it is printed together with the name. Grades are assigned as follows:

mark >= 80:	Distinction
mark between 65-79:	Merit
mark between 50 and 64:	Pass
mark < 50:	Fail

Local and global variables

Variables used in the main program are by default **global variables**, and these can be used anywhere in the program, including within any subroutines. Within a subroutine, **local variables** can be used and these exist only during the execution of the subroutine. They cannot be accessed outside the subroutine and changing them has no effect on any variable outside the subroutine, even if the variable happens to have the same name as the local variable.

1-5

Q7: Can you find a local variable in `SUB cylinderVolume(r,len)` in Example 3 above? What would happen if you tried to print its value in the main program?

The ability to declare local variables is very useful because it ensures that each subroutine is completely self-contained and independent of any global variables that have been declared in the main program. The principles of **data hiding** and **encapsulation** of all the variables needed in a subroutine are very important in programming. A subroutine written according to these principles can be tested independently, and used many times in many different programs without the programmer needing to know what variables it uses. Any variable in the calling program which coincidentally has the same name as a local variable declared in the subroutine will not cause an unexpected side-effect.

Example 4

```
1   SUB printNumbers(x)
2       a ← 1
3       b ← 2
4       c ← 3
5       OUTPUT "In the subroutine, a,b,c and x have values ", a,b,c,x
6   ENDSUB

7   #main program
8   a ← 4
9   b ← 5
10  c ← 6
11  x ← 10
12  OUTPUT "In the main program, a,b,c and x have values ", a,b,c,x
13  printNumbers(x)
14  OUTPUT "In the main program, a,b,c and x now have values ", a,b,c,x
```

Q8: Write down the line numbers of the statements in the order in which they are executed.

Q9: What will be the output of the program?

Q10: What will happen when the following program is run?

```
SUB printnum
    y ← 20
    OUTPUT "In sub printnum, y = ", y
ENDSUB
#main program
printnum
OUTPUT "In main program, y = ", y
```

Modular programming

When a program is short and simple, there is no need to break it up into subroutines. With a long, complex program, however, a 'top-down' approach, in which the problem is broken down into a number of subtasks, is generally very helpful in designing the algorithm for reaching a satisfactory solution.

Programming with subroutines

Using subroutines in a large program has many advantages:

- A subroutine is small enough to be understandable as a unit of code. It is therefore relatively easy to understand, debug and maintain especially if its purpose is clearly defined and documented
- Subroutines can be tested independently, thereby shortening the time taken to get a large program working
- Once a subroutine has been thoroughly tested, it can be reused with confidence in different programs or parts of the same program
- In a very large project, several programmers may be working on a single program. Using a modular approach, each programmer can be given a specific set of subroutines to work on. This enables the whole program to be finished sooner
- A large project becomes easier to monitor and control

Example 5

A program is to be written which simulates a dice game in which 2 players take turns. The rules of the game are as follows:

Players take turns to throw two dice. If the throw is a 'double', i.e. two 2s, two 3s, etc., the player's score reverts to zero and their turn ends. If the throw is not a 'double', the total shown on the two dice is added to the player's score. A player may have as many throws as they like in any turn until they either throw a double or pass the dice. The first player to reach a score of 50 wins the game.

We will design the solution in a top-down manner. A first attempt at listing the major tasks to be performed might be:

```
REPEAT
    display the menu (display rules, play game or quit)
    get the user's choice (1 to display rules, 2 to play, 3 to quit)
    call a routine to either display the rules, play the game or quit
UNTIL the user chooses quit
OUTPUT "Goodbye"
```

1-5

The major tasks can be split into subroutines, which can each be tested independently.

We need the following subroutines:

```
SUB   menuChoice       #display menu and get user's choice
SUB   displayRules
SUB   playGame
```

Playing the game needs to be broken down further. At this stage we can start writing pseudocode for a subroutine playGame which will do the following:

```
SUB  playGame
    initialise scores of each player (score1 and score2) to zero
    ask for the players' names (player1 and player1)
    WHILE score1 < 50 AND score2 < 50
        score1 ← playerTurn(player1,score1)        # player 1's turn
        IF score1 >= 50 THEN
           OUTPUT "You win!"
        ELSE
           score2 ← playerTurn(player2,score2)        # player 2's turn
           IF score2 >= 50 THEN
              OUTPUT "You win!"
           ENDIF
        ENDIF
    ENDWHILE
ENDSUB
```

Finally, we have to design the subroutine `playerTurn`. This is incorporated into the pseudocode for the whole program, which is given below. In some languages it may be necessary to import a library containing the `random` function.

Q11: Have a go at writing an algorithm for `playerTurn` before you look at it! Alternatively, code the program in a language of your choice.

```
#program to play a 2-player dice game

SUB menuChoice
    OUTPUT "Option 1: Display rules"
    OUTPUT "Option 2: Start new game"
    OUTPUT "Option 3: Quit"
    OUTPUT "What would you like to do?"
    choice ← USERINPUT
    WHILE choice < 1 OR choice > 3
        OUTPUT "That is not a valid choice."
        OUTPUT "Please enter a number between 1 and 3: "
        choice ← USERINPUT
    ENDWHILE
    RETURN choice
ENDSUB
```

1-5

```
#subroutine to display rules

SUB displayRules
   OUTPUT "The rules of the game are as follows:
   Players take turns to throw two dice.
   If the throw is a 'double', i.e. two 2s, two 3s, etc.,
   the player's score reverts to zero and their turn ends.
   (etc.)"
ENDSUB


#subroutine for each player to take a turn

SUB playerTurn(player,score)
   OUTPUT "Your turn, ", player
   anotherGo ← "Y"
   scoreThisTurn ← 0
   WHILE anotherGo = "Y" OR anotherGo = "y"
      die1 ← random(1,6)   #call a built-in function
      die2 ← random(1,6)
      OUTPUT "You rolled ", die1," and", die2
      IF die1 = die2
         scoreThisTurn ← 0
         cumulativeScore ← 0
         OUTPUT "Bad luck! Press any key to continue"
         anyKey ← USERINPUT   #accept any keypress from user
         anotherGo ← "N"
      ELSE
         scoreThisTurn ← scoreThisTurn + die1 + die2
         cumulativeScore ← score + scoreThisTurn
         OUTPUT "Your score this turn is ",scoreThisTurn
         OUTPUT player,"Your cumulative score is ", cumulativeScore
         IF cumulativeScore >= 50 THEN
            anotherGo ← "N"
         ELSE
            OUTPUT "Another go? (Answer Y or N)"
            anotherGo ← USERINPUT
         ENDIF
      ENDIF
   ENDWHILE
   RETURN cumulativeScore
ENDSUB
```

```
#subroutine to play game
SUB playGame
    score1 ← 0
    score2 ← 0
    OUTPUT "Enter Player 1's name: "
    player1 ← USERINPUT
    OUTPUT "Enter Player 2's name: "
    player2 ← USERINPUT
    WHILE score1 < 50 AND score2 < 50
        score1 ← playerTurn(player1, score1)
        IF score1 >= 50 THEN
            OUTPUT "You win!"
        ELSE
            score2 ← playerTurn(player2, score2)
            IF score2 >= 50 THEN
                OUTPUT "You win!"
            ENDIF
        ENDIF
    ENDWHILE
ENDSUB

#main program starts here
option ← menuChoice
WHILE option <> 3
    IF option = 1 THEN
        displayRules
    ELSE
        playGame
    ENDIF
    option ← menuChoice
ENDWHILE
OUTPUT "Goodbye!"
```

1-5

Exercises

1. Referring to the program code above, answer the following questions.

    (a) Give **one** example of a global variable and **one** example of a local variable used in this program. Why is it good practice to use local variables whenever possible? [4]

    (b) Give **one** example of a parameter in this program. What is the advantage of using subroutines with parameters? [3]

    (c) The first statement in the main program is `option ← menuChoice`

    Explain what this statement does. [2]

Chapter 6 – Files and exception handling

Objectives

- define the terms field, record, file
- be able to read from and write to a text file
- understand when and how to use exception handling in a program

Fields, records and files

If you want to store data permanently so that you can read or update it at a future date, the data needs to be stored in a file on disk. The most common way of storing large amounts of data conveniently is to use a database, but sometimes you need to create and interrogate your own files.

Generally, a **file** consists of a number of **records**. A record contains a number of **fields**, each holding one item of data. For example, in a file holding data about students, you might have the following record structure:

ID	Firstname	Surname	DateOfBirth	Class
1453	Gemma	Baines	01/05/2004	2G
1768	Paul	Gerrard	17/11/2003	2G
2016	Brian	Davidson	03/08/2002	3H

The table shows a file containing three records, each record having 5 fields. In some languages, a record structure will be declared in the following manner:

```
Student = Record
   integer ID
   string Firstname
   string Surname
   date DateOfBirth
   string Class
End Record
```

This is an example of a user-defined data type.

Another way of storing a file is to use a **text file,** described below.

Writing to a text file

Suppose that you want to write to a text file containing the names of birds seen and the numbers of each bird reported by an individual participating in the RSPB's Big Garden Birdwatch described in Chapter 4, page 17. You may be starting a new file or appending data to an existing file – there are different 'modes' in which a file can be opened including read, write and append. We will assume that if you open the file in 'append' mode it will create a file if one does not already exist in the folder.

> **Q1:** Assume the user did not know how many records needed to be written to the file. Rewrite the pseudocode below so that it works for any number of records.

Programming languages have different syntax for writing to and reading from a file, but pseudocode for a program to write data to a new file would be something like the following:

```
OPEN birdFile to append data
OUTPUT "How many records do you wish to write?"
numRecs ← USERINPUT
FOR n ← 1 TO numRecs
   OUTPUT "Enter bird name: "
   birdName ← USERINPUT
   OUTPUT "Enter number of birds reported: "
   birdsReported ← USERINPUT
   WRITELINE (birdFile, birdName + birdsReported)
ENDFOR
CLOSE birdFile
```

Reading from a text file

Some programming languages such as Python will allow you to read an entire text file using just a single statement. You can also read a text file line by line (or record by record). Each record will have a number of fields commonly separated by commas, as in a CSV (comma-separated values) file.

Suppose you want to search `birdFile` for a specific bird name and print out the number of birds. Assume that this file has 8 records.

```
OPEN birdFile for reading
OUTPUT "What bird are you searching for? "
birdNameSearch ← USERINPUT
FOR n ← 1 TO 8
   READLINE (birdFile, n)                    #read the nth record
   Split record into individual comma-separated fields
   birdName ← field[0]
   birdsSeen ← field[1]
   IF birdName = birdNameSearch THEN
      OUTPUT birdName, birdsSeen
   ENDIF
ENDFOR
CLOSE birdFile
```

Q2: What does the following pseudocode do?
```
OPEN birdFile for reading
totalBirdsSeen ← 0
FOR n = 1 TO 8
   READLINE (birdFile, n)                    #read the nth record
   Split record into individual comma-separated fields
   birdsSeen ← int(field[1])                 #convert string to integer
   totalBirdsSeen ← totalBirdsSeen + birdsSeen
ENDFOR
OUTPUT "Total birds seen: ", totalBirdsSeen
CLOSE birdFile
```

1-6

Overwriting text in an existing file

Sometimes you may want to overwrite existing data; for example, to correct a record in the file. In that case, you can open the record for both reading and writing, search through the file for the record you want, and write a new record in its place.

Binary (non-text) files

It is possible to read and write binary files as well as text files. A binary file can contain records with different types of field such as string, integer, real, Boolean. Each of these fields may occupy a different number of bytes; for example a real number stored as text may occupy 12 bytes for a 12-figure number, but considerably fewer as a pure binary number.

Reading a binary file is language-specific but always involves knowing exactly what each field type in the record is and how many bytes it occupies. The file needs to be opened in a mode which specifies that it is a binary file.

Exception handling

It is a good idea to include in your programs some exception-handling routines to specify what should happen if an error occurs that would normally cause the program to crash. Common errors of this sort include:

- trying to read a non-existent file

- trying to convert a non-numeric string entered by the user, to an integer or a real number

- trying to perform calculations with a non-numeric variable

- division by zero

Most languages provide an easy way of handling exceptions with a try...except clause. Here are three examples:

Example 1

```
TRY
   OPEN birdFile for reading
EXCEPT
   OUTPUT ("Sorry, can't find this file")
ENDEXCEPT
```

Example 2

Below is an example of a validation routine that could be used in the program shown in the last chapter to simulate a simple dice game.

> **Q3:** What will be displayed by this subroutine if the user enters the following?
> (i) 4   (ii) e

1-6

```
SUB menuChoice
   OUTPUT "Option 1: Display rules"
   OUTPUT "Option 2: Start new game"
   OUTPUT "Option 3: Quit"
   OUTPUT "What would you like to do? "
   choice ← USERINPUT
   WHILE choice < "1" OR choice > "3"
      TRY
         choiceAsInteger ← int(choice) #try to convert string to integer
      EXCEPT
         OUTPUT "That is not an integer!"
      ENDEXCEPT
      # The user entry may be an integer but not between 1 and 3…
      OUTPUT "Please try again… enter a number between 1 and 3: "
      choice ← USERINPUT
   ENDWHILE
   RETURN choiceAsInteger
ENDSUB
```

Example 3

This example shows the use of TRY… EXCEPT… ELSE.

```
n ← 10
TRY
   birdRec = READLINE(birdFile, n)
EXCEPT
   OUTPUT "Attempt to read beyond end of file"
ELSE
   Split record into individual comma-separated fields
   TRY
      birdsSeen ← int(field[1])  #convert string to integer
   EXCEPT
      birdsSeen = 0
      OUTPUT "This is not an integer"
   ELSE
      totalBirdsSeen ← totalBirdsSeen + birdsSeen
   ENDEXCEPT
ENDEXCEPT
```

Exercises

1. Write pseudocode for a program which reads a text file containing the current highest score for a game. Compare the current highest with a variable called `myscore` and if `myscore` is greater than the one on the file, replace the record with the new high score. [5]

2. (a) Explain with the aid of an example, the purpose of exception-handling in programs involving file handling. [2]

   (b) Explain why exception-handling routines are useful for validating data input by the user.

   [3]

Section 2

Problem solving and theory of computation

In this section:

2

Chapter 7 – Solving logic problems

Objectives

- Define the stages of systems development
- Be able to develop solutions to simple logic problems
- Be able to check solutions to simple logic problems

Stages in software development

Software is the name given to any program written for the computer.

There are several well-defined stages in writing software, once your programs progress past the trivial and become more challenging. The stages are:

Briefly, the tasks performed at each of these stages are:

- **Analysis:** the requirements and goals of the project must be established, and a data model created. The needs of the end user are considered, and alternative solutions to the problem may be suggested

- **Design:** data structures will be specified, algorithms, user interfaces, screen designs and reports will all be designed

- **Implementation:** the program code is written

- **Testing:** the whole system must be tested for the presence of errors, using selected test data covering normal, boundary and erroneous data

- **Evaluation:** the system is evaluated according to given criteria

It is not necessary or even desirable that one phase is finished before another starts. In an evolutionary prototyping approach, some parts of the design, such as the user interface, may be implemented and shown to the customer, who then gives feedback. If it is not what they wanted, further work is done on the design. Testing may begin on parts of the implementation before other parts are completed. At each stage, it may be necessary to revisit previous stages. Customer feedback at every stage is crucial for successful project development.

We will go through the first four of these stages in this Section, starting with some problem-solving exercises which will get you thinking creatively about how to solve problems – a useful skill for analysing a problem and designing a solution. The types of problems we will be looking at are "computational" rather than "data-processing" problems.

Problem-solving

Solving logic problems is good training for "computational thinking" – basically, the ability to think logically about a problem and apply techniques for solving it. This is closely related to the skill of designing algorithms which can be turned into computer programs.

This chapter is designed to get you thinking about developing and checking solutions to simple logic problems.

(Solutions to the example problems are given at the end of the chapter.)

One type of problem asks you to find a method of solving a problem which has a goal and a set of resources, as in Question 1.

Q1: There are two jugs, A and B. Jug A has a capacity of three litres. Jug B has a capacity of five litres. There are no markings on the jugs, so it is not possible to tell exactly how much is in a jug just by looking at it, unless it is full or empty. There is a sink with a water tap and a drain. How can exactly one litre of water be obtained from the tap using the two jugs?

Tip: Create a table like the one below with 3 columns headed **Step, A (3 litres), B (5 litres)**, and several blank rows. Write the contents of each jug after each step.

Step	A (3 litres)	B (5 litres)
1	3	0
2	etc	

Some problems require you to work out a method of solution and use the clues to find the answer, as in the following problem. An example of this type of problem is shown below.

Q2: The police are interrogating five suspects after a bank robbery. Each of them makes two statements, but it turns out only five of these statements are true.

Can you work out who committed the crime? What strategy will you use to work it out?

Alan said: It wasn't Ben. It was Carl.

Ben said: It wasn't Alan. It was Dave.

Carl said: It wasn't Dave. It wasn't Ben, either.

Dave said: It wasn't Eddie. It was Alan.

Eddie said: It wasn't Carl. It was Derek.

Tip: What is the key fact given in the statement of the problem?

2-7

Example 3 is a classic logic problem, which has many different variations on the same theme.

Q3: A man has to get a fox, a chicken, and a sack of corn across a river.

He has a rowing boat, which can carry only him and one other thing.

If the fox and the chicken are left together, the fox will eat the chicken.

If the chicken and the corn are left together, the chicken will eat the corn.

How does the man do it?

Strategies for problem solving

There are some general strategies for designing algorithms which are useful for solving many problems in computer science. First of all it is useful to note that there are two types of algorithmic puzzle. Every puzzle has an **input**, which defines an **instance** of the puzzle. The instance can be either **specific** (e.g. fill a magic square with 3 rows and 3 columns), or **general** (n rows and n columns). Even when given a general instance of a problem, it is often helpful to solve a specific instance of it, which may give an insight into solving a more general case.

Exhaustive search

For example, suppose you are asked to fill a 'magic square' with 3 rows and 3 columns with distinct integers 1-9 so that the sum of the numbers in each row, column and corner-to-corner diagonal is the same.

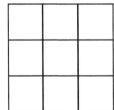

This is a **specific** instance of a more **general** problem in which there are n rows and n columns. Some problems can be solved by **exhaustive search** – in this example, by trying every possible combination of numbers. We can put any one of 9 integers in the first square, and any of the remaining 8 in the second square, giving 9x8 = 72 possibilities for just the first two squares. There are 9x8x7x6x5x4x3x2 = 362,880 ways of filling the square. If you are a mathematician you will know that this is denoted by 9!, spoken as "nine factorial".

You might think a computer could do this in a fraction of a second. However, looking at the more general problem, where you have n x n squares, you will find that even for a 5 x 5 square, there are so many different combinations (25! or 25 factorial) that it would take a computer performing 10 trillion operations a second, about 49,000 years to find the answer!

So, to solve this problem we need to come up with a better algorithm. It turns out to be not very difficult to work out that for a 3 x 3 square, each row, column and diagonal must add up to 15 and the middle number must be 5, which considerably reduces the size of the problem. (The details of the algorithm are not discussed here.)

Q4: Fill the magic square to solve the problem.

Divide-and-conquer

To find a particular item in a sorted list, one strategy is to look at every item starting from the beginning until you find what you are looking for (the **exhaustive** search strategy). A far more efficient strategy is to perform a **binary search**:

Step 1: Look at the middle item of the list first. If this is the item being sought, stop searching

Step 2: Otherwise, if the middle item is greater than the one being sought, the item you are looking for must be in the first half of the list so you can discard the second half. Otherwise, discard the first half of the list

Step 3: Repeat with the new list until the item is found.

> **Q5:** Ask a friend to think of a number between 1 and 20. You have a guess and your friend tells you whether it is correct, too low or too high. What is the maximum number of guesses you will need with the best algorithm as described above?
>
> How many guesses, at worst, will you need to find a number between 1 and 1000?
>
> How many guesses, at worst, for a number between 1 and 2^n?
>
> How many guesses, at worst, using the "exhaustive search" strategy?

Sometimes a problem requires a flash of insight to solve. If you have seen the film "The Imitation Game" about Alan Turing and how he cracked the Enigma Code during World War II, you will recall his insight in realising that most messages ended with the words "Heil Hitler". This proved crucial in reducing the exhaustive search algorithm, which could never provide the solution in the 24 hours before the code was changed, to one which the code-breakers used to decode the messages every day.

2-7

> **Q6:** You have a bag of 8 coins which all look identical, but one of them is counterfeit and weighs less than a genuine coin.
> You have a two-pan balance, but no weights.
>
> What is the minimum number of weighings needed to identify the fake coin?
>
> *Tip:* The answer is not 3 weighings!

Solutions to examples

Q1: Fill the 3-litre jug and pour it into the 5-litre jug. Then refill the 3-litre jug and pour 2 litres into the 5-litre jug to fill it. What remains in the 3-litre jug is 1 litre.

Q2: If Alan did it, that means that 6 of the statements are true. Try out each person in turn. Eddie is the only one who fits the criterion that exactly 5 statements are true. (This is the key fact.)

Q3: The man and the chicken cross the river, (the fox and corn are safe together). He leaves the chicken on the other side and goes back across.

The man then takes the fox across the river, and since he can't leave the fox and chicken together, he takes the chicken back with him.

Then, since the chicken and corn can't be left together, he leaves the chicken and he takes the corn across and leaves it with the fox.

He then returns to pick up the chicken and heads across the river one last time.

Solutions to examples continued

Q4: Here is one solution…

2	7	6
9	5	1
4	3	8

Q5: You will need up to 5 guesses; 20 is more than 2^4 and less than 2^5. You will need a maximum of 10 guesses to find a number between 1 and 1000, since 1000 is greater than 2^9 and less than 2^{10}.

Taking the general case, you will need a maximum of n guesses to guess a number between 1 and 2^n.

Q6: Select two groups of three coins each and weigh them against each other. If they weigh the same, weigh the other two and the lighter will be identified. If not, the lighter coin will be among the three in the lighter pan. Weigh two of these. If they are the same, the third is the counterfeit coin. If they do not weigh the same, the lighter one is the counterfeit.

Exercises

2-7

1. Three days ago, yesterday was the day before Sunday. What day will it be tomorrow?

2. There are two married couples who need to cross a river. They have a boat that can hold no more than two people at a time. The husbands insist that at no time can their wives be left alone in the company of the other man. How can they cross the river?

3. You have an 8-pint jug full of water, and two empty jugs of 5- and 3-pint capacity. How can you get exactly 4 pints of water into one of the jugs by completely filling up and/or emptying jugs into others?

4. The following problem has become very popular since it is reputed to have been set to candidates during job interviews at Microsoft.

   A group of four people, who have one torch between them, need to cross a rickety bridge at night. A maximum of two people can cross the bridge at one time, and any party that crosses (either one or two people) must have the torch with them. The torch must be walked back and forth – it cannot be thrown. Person A takes one minute to cross the bridge, person B takes 2 minutes, person C takes 5 minutes and person D takes 10 minutes. A pair must walk together at the rate of the slower person's pace.

   Find the fastest way they can accomplish this task.

Chapter 8 – Structured programming

Objectives

- understand the structured approach to program design and construction
- be able to construct and use hierarchy charts when designing programs
- be able to explain the advantages of the structured approach

The structured approach

The structured programming approach aims to improve the **clarity** and **maintainability** of programs. (See Chapter 5, page 25, "Programming with subroutines".) Using structured programming techniques, only three basic programming structure are used:

- sequence – one statement following another
- selection – IF … THEN … ELSE… ENDIF and CASE … ENDCASE statements
- iteration – WHILE … ENDWHILE, REPEAT… UNTIL and FOR … ENDFOR loops

Languages such as Python, Pascal and C# are **block-structured languages** which allow the use of just three types of control structure. They may allow you to break out of a loop, but this is not recommended in structured programming. Each block should have a single entry and exit point.

Block-structured languages

A block is a section of code consisting of one or more statements. For example, a block may be a single IF … ENDIF statement, with the beginning of the block denoted by, for example, the keyword IF or an opening curly bracket, and the end denoted by either the end of indented code, (as in Python), a curly bracket or a keyword such as END or ENDIF.

A block may also be a subroutine such as a **function** or **procedure**. Another important aspect of structured programming is to keep subroutines independent of the program which calls them, which means that they should not make use of global variables. Any variable declared in the main program should be passed as a parameter to a subroutine if it is needed.

2-8

> **Q1:** Why is it important for clarity not to use global variables in subroutines?

Designing structured programs

Top-down design is the technique of breaking down a problem into the major tasks to be performed; each of these tasks is then further broken down into separate subtasks, and so on until each subtask is sufficiently simple to be written as a self-contained **module** or subroutine. Remember that some programs contain tens of thousands, or even millions, of lines of code, and a strategy for design is absolutely essential. Even for small programs, top-down design is a very useful method of breaking down the problem into small, manageable tasks.

> **Q2:** A computer scientist named Tom Harbron stated: "The Fundamental Principle of Structured Programming is that at all times and under all circumstances, the programmer must keep the program within his intellectual grasp. The well-known methods for achieving this can be briefly summarised as follows: 1) top-down design and construction, 2) limited control structures, and 3) limited scope of data structures." Discuss what he meant by this statement.

Advantages of structured (modular) programming

The advantages of thes structured approach may be stated as:

- Individual modules can be separately tested
- Modules can be kept in a module library and reused in other programs
- Large programs can be split into modules that are easier to read, debug and maintain
- Several programmers in a team can work on separate modules, thus shortening development time for a large project

Hierarchy charts

A hierarchy chart is a tool for representing the structure of a program, showing how the modules relate to each other to form the complete solution. The chart is depicted as an upside-down tree structure, with modules being broken down further into smaller modules until each module is only a few lines of code (never more than a page).

Example 1

Draw a hierarchy chart for a program which calculates and prints a customer's monthly gas bill.

This can be broken down into several steps.

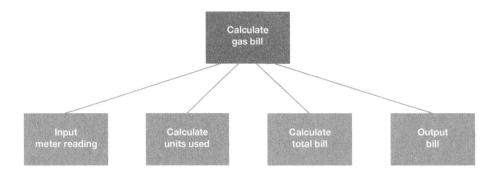

'Calculate units used' and *'Calculate total bill'* may now be further broken down.

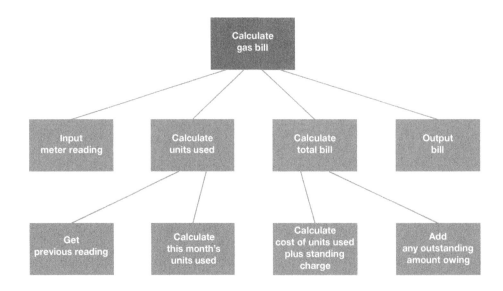

2-8

Limitations of a hierarchy chart

Note that a hierarchy chart does not show the detailed program structures required in each module – for example, it does not show selection and iteration. A greater level of detail may be shown in a **structure chart** but these are not covered here.

Example 2

Draw a hierarchy chart for a program which asks the user which times table they would like to be tested on, and then displays five questions, getting the user's answer each time and telling them whether they were right or wrong. If they are wrong, the correct answer is displayed.

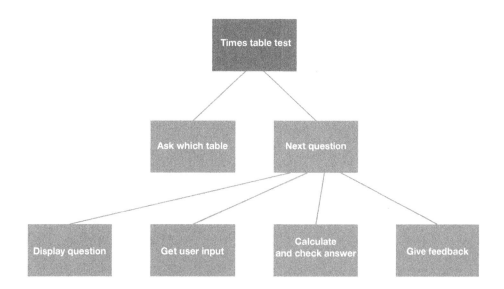

Q3: Draw a hierarchy chart for the program given in Q11 in Chapter 5, page 26.

Exercises

1. Using local rather than global variables in subroutines is one way of helping to make a program easy to maintain.

   (i) Explain why this is the case. [3]

   (ii) Describe briefly **three** other ways in which a program can be made easy to understand and maintain. [6]

2. Draw a hierarchy chart for a quiz program which does the following:

   • asks the user 10 random multiple-choice questions from a bank of 100 questions held in a file

   • if the user gives the correct answer, gives feedback and adds 1 to the user's score

   • if they give the wrong answer, gives feedback and displays the correct answer

   • at the end of the questions, gives the score out of 10

   • asks if they want another 10 questions [6]

Chapter 9 – Writing and interpreting algorithms

Objectives

- To understand the term 'algorithm'
- To learn how to write and interpret algorithms using pseudocode

Properties of an algorithm

A recipe for chocolate cake, a knitting pattern for a sweater or a set of directions to get from A to B, are all algorithms of a kind.

Computational algorithms

The definition of an algorithm is:

- It has clear and precisely stated steps that produce the correct output for any set of valid inputs
- It must always terminate at some point

A good algorithm also has the following properties:

- It should allow for invalid inputs
- It should execute efficiently, in as few steps as possible
- It should be designed in such a way that other people will be able to understand it and modify it if necessary

What kinds of problem are solved by algorithms?

There are thousands of different practical applications of algorithms. Some of the best-known applications include:

- **Internet-related algorithms**. Algorithms are used to manage and manipulate the huge amount of data stored on the Internet. How does a search engine find all the pages on which particular information resides in a fraction of a second?

- **Route-finding algorithms**. Given two locations, how does a route-finder determine the shortest or best route between the two points? There may be thousands of possible routes. This type of algorithm is used not only for driving a vehicle from A to B, but also for many other applications, for example, finding the best route to transmit packets of data from A to B over a network.

- **Compression algorithms**. These are used to compress data files so that they can be transmitted faster or held in a smaller amount of storage space. For example, MP3 files are compressed so that you can hold thousands of tracks on a mobile phone.

- **Encryption algorithms**. When someone purchases something over the Internet and sends their credit card number and other personal details to the store, the data needs to be encrypted so that even if it is intercepted, it cannot be read.

Q1: Who else uses encryption algorithms?

A simple computational algorithm

Suppose you are given the square of an integer and you need to find the integer itself (i.e. the square root of the given number). Your calculator can add, subtract, multiply and divide but it does not have a square root function.

Here is one way of finding the square root of the integer `number`:

```
1  n ← 0                        ;initialise n
2  nsquared ← n*n
3  Is nsquared = number?
4  If yes, output n. If no, add 1 to n and repeat from step 2
```

When you start to program, it is tempting to get straight to the computer and type in some code to solve a given problem. However, it will generally save time to figure out the steps needed using paper and pencil before you start coding using **pseudocode**.

Pseudocode is a way of expressing the solution in a way that can easily be translated into a programming language.

Q2: Write pseudocode for the above algorithm to find the square root of an integer, when you know that the answer is an integer. Write and test the program for the integer 19321.

Q3: Which of the properties of a good algorithm, stated at the start of the chapter, does this algorithm not satisfy?

The algorithm described will do the job, but a better solution is based on the well-known binary search algorithm, which we looked at briefly in Chapter 7, Question 5.

2-9

A "Divide and Conquer" algorithm

This algorithm uses the "Divide and Conquer" strategy to halve the search area every time a guess is made. It goes like this:

1. Set `low ← 1, high ← number, guess ← (low + high)/2` and `nsquared ← guess`^{2}

2. If `nsquared > number`, set `high ← guess` to eliminate the top half of the range, otherwise set `low ← guess` to eliminate the bottom half of the range

3. Set `guess ← (low + high)/2` and `nsquared ← guess`^{2}

4. Repeat steps 2 and 3 until `nsquared = number`

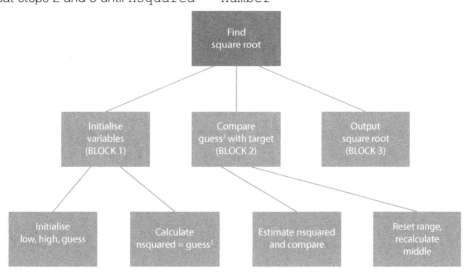

The chart represents the blocks of program code that we will use to solve the problem. The solution is short, so it's not necessary to put each block in a separate subroutine.

```
number ← 19321
low ← 1
high ← number
guess ← int((low + high) / 2)
nsquared ← guess ** 2                              BLOCK 1 SEQUENCE
```

```
WHILE nsquared <> number
   IF nsquared > number THEN
      high ← guess
   ELSE
      low ← guess
   ENDIF
   guess ← int((low + high) / 2)
   nsquared ← guess ** 2                           BLOCK 2 - ITERATION
ENDWHILE
```

```
OUTPUT "Square root is ",guess                     BLOCK 3 - SEQUENCE
```

2-9

Q4: Add statements to calculate and print the number of guesses it took to find the answer.

Try writing and running the program for different values of xsquared.

Is there a formula for calculating how many guesses it should take to find the square root?

Sorting algorithms

Sorting is a very common task in data processing, and frequently the number of items may be huge, so using a good algorithm can considerably reduce the time spent on the task. There are many efficient sorting algorithms such as quicksort and merge sort but you will not be required to use these in this course, so we will look at a simple but rather inefficient sort algorithm as an example.

Bubble sort

The Bubble sort is one of the most basic sorting algorithms and the simplest to understand. The basic idea is to bubble up the largest (or smallest) item, then the second largest, then the third largest and so on until no more swaps are needed.

Suppose you have an array of n items:

- Go through the array, comparing each item with the one next to it. If it is greater, swap them.

- The last item in the array will be in the correct place after the first pass

- Repeat n - 1 times, reducing by one on each pass, the number of items to be examined

Q5: How do you swap two items in an array?

Example 1

Write pseudocode for a bubble sort to sort the numbers 45, 62, 13, 98, 9, 50 into ascending sequence. Print the numbers after each of the 6 passes through the list.

```
numbers ← [45,62,13,98,9,50]
numItems ← len(numbers)        #get number of items in the array
FOR i ← 0 TO numItems - 2
   FOR j ← 0 TO numItems - i - 2
      IF numbers[j] > numbers[j + 1] THEN
         # Swap the numbers in the array
            temp ← numbers[j]
            numbers[j] ← numbers[j + 1]
            numbers[j + 1] ← temp
      ENDIF
   ENDFOR
   OUTPUT numbers
ENDFOR
```

If you run this program, the output is

[45, 13, 62, 9, 50, 98]

[13, 45, 9, 50, 62, 98]

[13, 9, 45, 50, 62, 98]

[9, 13, 45, 50, 62, 98]

[9, 13, 45, 50, 62, 98]

Q6: Describe how you could modify this algorithm to make it more efficient when there is a large number of items to be sorted.

2-9

Interpreting programs

A useful skill is to be able to look at someone else's program and decide what it does and how it works. Of course, if the programmer has put in lots of useful comments, used meaningful variable names and split a complicated program into separate modules, that should not be too difficult!

Strategy for interpreting programs

Here are some tips, which may seem fairly obvious.

1. Read the comments in the program

2. Look at the variable names to see if they give any clues

3. Follow the steps in the program – the one below starts with the statement shift ← 3

4. Try a "dry run" with some test data

Evaluating a program

When two programs written to solve the same problem are not the same, is one program better than the other? It may be that one program is well documented with comments, uses meaningful variable names and properly indented code, does not contain statements that are not needed, and uses a more efficient algorithm. Once a program has been written and tested, you need to be able to:

- articulate how it works
- produce test data and results to show that it works correctly
- get user feedback to show that nothing has been omitted, that it performs all the required tasks and does so efficiently

Q7: What will be the output from the algorithm below if the user inputs "Hi, Jo!"

Explain briefly the purpose of the algorithm.

```
SUB code(message, shift)
   message ← lowercase(message)
   codedMessage ← ""
   FOR x IN message
      IF x IN "abcdefghijklmnopqrstuvwxyz" THEN
         num ← ord(x)                 # convert to ASCII value
         num ← num + shift
         IF num > ord("z") THEN       # wrap if necessary
            num ← num - 26
         ENDIF
         char ← chr(num)              # convert back to character
         codedMessage ← codedMessage + char
      ELSE
         codedMessage ← codedMessage + x
      ENDIF
   ENDFOR
   RETURN codedMessage
ENDSUB


# main program
shift ← 3
OUTPUT("Enter your message: ")
msg ← USERINPUT
codedMessage ← code(msg,shift)
OUTPUT("The encoded message is: ", codedMessage)
```

2-9

Exercises

1. (a) Three types of programming constructs are sequence, selection and iteration.

Describe what is meant by each of these. [6]

(b) A computer program contains the following instructions:

```
X ← 10
Y ← 20
X ← Y
OUTPUT X, Y
```

    (i) State which of the constructs in part (a) has been used. [1]

    (ii) What will be output by this code? [1]

2. In a football league, the results of each match are input to the computer, which updates each team's points.

In the case of a draw, each team (Team A and Team B) gets one point.

If Team A wins, then Team A gets 3 points and Team B gets no points.

The algorithm for updating points in the case of a draw is:

```
IF TeamAGoals = TeamBGoals THEN
    TeamAPoints ← TeamAPoints + 1
    TeamBPoints ← TeamBPoints + 1
ENDIF
```

Write an algorithm for updating the points if there is a winner. [3]

2-9

3. Expert jugglers learn new juggling patterns according to certain rules represented by numbers. In this example, the rules for patterns of three numbers are:

Rule 1: the total value of the numbers in the list must be a multiple of 3

Rule 2: No number must be one less than the previous number, even if the pattern
      is repeated indefinitely.

Here are some valid patterns of three numbers:

    7 4 4

    4 4 1

Here are some examples of invalid patterns with three numbers:

    4 2 1   (4 + 2 + 1 = 7, which is not a multiple of 3, so does not obey rule 1)

    6 5 1   (5 is one less than the previous number, so this does not obey rule 2)

    6 2 7   (when this is repeated, 6 2 7 6 2 7 6 2 7... 6 is one less than the previous number,
            so this does not obey rule 2)

(a) State why the following lists of 3 numbers are not valid patterns of numbers.

    (i) 5 1 6 [1]

    (ii) 4 4 2 [1]

(b) Write pseudocode for a program which:

    • Prompts the user to enter 3 numbers, one after the other

    • Outputs "INVALID PATTERN" if the sequence of numbers does not obey the two rules. [7]

Chapter 10 – Testing and evaluation

Objectives

- Understand the purpose of testing

- Devise a test plan

- Select test data covering normal (typical), boundary and erroneous data

- Check an algorithm by completing a dry run

- Know the criteria for evaluating a system

The purpose of testing

We have looked briefly at problem-solving strategies and the design of solutions using structured programming techniques. You will have implemented several algorithms in your practical sessions. **Testing** your solutions for correctness can be a complex and time-consuming task, but one that needs to be done thoroughly and systematically.

The purpose of testing is not to show that your program usually works correctly, if the user is careful when entering input data. ***The purpose of testing is to try and uncover undetected errors.***

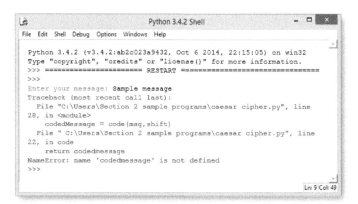

Devising a test plan

Your program should work correctly whatever data is input. If invalid data is entered, the program should detect and report this, and ask the user to enter valid data. Some data may be valid, but may nevertheless cause the program to crash if you have not allowed for particular values.

We need to choose test data that will test the outcome for any user input. To do this, we need to select **normal**, **boundary** and **erroneous** data.

- **normal** data is data within the range that you would expect, and of the data type (real, integer, string, etc.) that you would expect. For example, if you are expecting an input between 0 and 100, you should test 1 and 99

- **boundary** data is data at the ends of the expected range or just either side of it – for example -1, 0, 1, 99, 100, 101. Test 0 and 100 to make sure that these give the expected results if the valid range is between 0 and 100

- **erroneous** data is data that is either outside an expected range, e.g. -1, 101 or is of the wrong data type – for example, non-numeric characters when you are expecting a number to be input

For each test, you should specify the purpose of the test, the expected result and the actual result.

Example 1

The following program is intended to calculate and print the average mark for each student in a class, for all the tests they have attempted:

```
OUTPUT "How many students? "
students ← USERINPUT
FOR n ← 1 TO students
    OUTPUT "Enter student name"
    name ← USERINPUT
    OUTPUT "Enter total marks for ", name
    totalMarks ← USERINPUT
    OUTPUT "How many tests has this student taken? "
    numTests ← USERINPUT
    averageMark ← ROUND(totalMarks/numTests)
    OUTPUT "Average mark ",averageMark
ENDFOR
```

The test plan will look something like this:

Test number	Test data	Purpose of test	Expected result	Actual result
1	Number of students = 4 for tests 1-4 Jo: total marks 27, tests 3	Normal data, integer result	9	9
2	Tom: total marks 31, tests 4	Normal data, non-integer result rounded up	8	8
3	Beth: total marks 28, tests 3	Normal data, result rounded down	9	9
4	Amina: total marks 0, tests 0	No tests taken	0	Program crashes
5	Number of students abc	Test invalid data	Program terminates	

You can probably think of some other input data that would make the program crash. For example, what if the user enters 31.5 for the total marks? The program should validate all user input, so some amendments will have to be made.

Q1: Devise a test plan for the program in Q7, page 46.

Dry-running a program

A useful technique to locate an error in a program is to perform a **dry run**, with the aid of a **trace table**. As you follow through the logic of the program in the same sequence as the computer does, you note down in the trace table when each variable changes and what its value is. Examples of this are given in the exercises below.

Evaluating a computer system

Once a system has been written and thoroughly tested, the final stage is **evaluation**. This will take place over a period of time, during which the user may run the new system in parallel to an old one. The criteria that may be used for evaluation include:

- Does it meet the performance criteria:
    - Can it handle the amount of data or users that it needs to in a live environment?
    - Is the speed of operation satisfactory?
- Does it always perform as expected?
- Is the system reliable or does it crash at intervals?
- Is the system easy to use?
- Is the interface pleasant to work with, all spellings correct, navigation simple and not 'clunky'?
- Has all the functionality documented in the original specification been implemented, or has one or more of the requirements been overlooked?
- Has it been well documented?
- Will it be easy to maintain?
- How far has the system been 'future-proofed' - will it be easy to upgrade or add new features in the future?
- How cost effective is the system - will it increase income, decrease costs, or both?

2-10

Exercises

1. Complete the trace table below to show how each variable changes when the algorithm is performed on the text data given.

```
x ← 0
y ← 0
z ← 0
w ← USERINPUT
REPEAT
    x ← x + w
    y ← y + 1
    w ← USERINPUT
UNTIL w < 0
z ← x / y
OUTPUT z
```

Test data: 5 7 2 2 4 -1   [5]

w	x	y	z
	0	0	0
5	5	1	0

2. Explain what is meant by an *algorithm*.   [2]

One way of checking that an algorithm is correct is to complete a dry run.
Dry run the algorithm below by completing the table below.   [6]

Assume that x has a value of 7. The MOD operator calculates the remainder resulting from an integer division.

```
Answer ← True
FOR Count ← 2 to (x-1) DO
    Remainder ← x MOD Count
    IF Remainder = 0 THEN
        Answer ← False
    ENDIF
ENDFOR
```

Answer	Count	Remainder
True	–	–
	2	1

What is the purpose of this algorithm?   [1]

AQA Comp 1 Qu 5 June 2010

2-10

Chapter 11 – Abstraction and automation

Objectives

- Describe the skills involved in computational thinking

- Understand the concept of abstraction

- Give examples of different types of abstraction

- Describe the process of automation for solving problems

Computational thinking

By this time, you are probably fairly clear about the idea of an algorithm and a problem which involves computation. But what is **computational thinking**? It is not about following an algorithm in one's head to carry out a mathematical task like adding two numbers. Rather, it is about thinking how a problem can be solved. This involves two basic steps:

- Formulate the problem as a computational problem – in other words, state it in such a way that it is potentially solvable using an algorithm

- Try to construct an algorithm to solve the problem

A computational thinker will not be satisfied with any old algorithm, though; it must be a 'good' solution – that is, a *correct* and *efficient* solution. A programmer needs to be able to show that a solution is correct and efficient by using logical reasoning, test data and user feedback.

Clearly, then, computational thinking is a vital skill for a programmer, and in fact it is not possible to be a programmer without it. It includes the ability to think logically and to apply the tools and techniques of computing to thinking about, understanding, formulating and solving problems.

Computing has been called the **automation of abstractions**, so let's move on to talk about abstraction.

Abstraction

Representational abstraction can be defined as *a representation arrived at by removing unnecessary details*.

Here are some examples of abstraction.

- Any computer model, say of the environment, a new car or a flight simulator, is an abstraction.

- If you are planning to write a program for a game involving a bouncing ball, you will need to decide what properties of the ball to take into account. If it's bouncing vertically rather than, say, on a snooker table, gravity needs to be taken into account. How elastic is the ball? How far and in what direction will it bounce when it hits an edge? What you are required to do is build an abstract model of a real-world situation, which you can simplify; remembering, however, that the more you simplify, the less likely it becomes that the model will mimic reality.

2-11

- A builder who is planning to build 100 houses on a new estate may use a physical model of the new estate, or in the first instance, a plan on paper or on a computer screen. In either case the model will be greatly simplified. All the houses may appear identical in the model. They may lack windows, doors or chimneys. All the trees in the model may be of identical size, colour and shape.

- The map of the London Underground is a simple model of the actual geography of the Tube stations. The map tells you what line each station is on and which other lines each station is connected to. It is very useful for a person travelling around London, but of very little use to an engineer who is planning where to dig tunnels for a proposed new line.

2-11

Abstraction applied to high level programming languages

Abstraction is the most important feature of high level programming languages such as Python, C#, Java and hundreds of other languages written for different purposes. To understand why, we need to look at different generations of programming language.

- The first generation of language was **machine code** – programmers entered the binary 0s and 1s that the computer understands. Writing a program to solve even a short, simple problem was a tedious, time-consuming task largely unrelated to the algorithm itself.

- The second generation was an improvement; mnemonic codes were used to represent instructions. But as you will see in later chapters in Sections 4 and 5, it was still an enormously complex task to write an assembly language program and what's more, if you wanted to run the program on a different type of computer, it had to be completely rewritten for the new hardware.

- The third generation of languages, starting with BASIC and FORTRAN in the 1960s, used statements like X = A + 5, finally freeing the programmer from all the tedious details of where the variables X and A were stored in memory, and all the other fiddly implementation details of exactly how the computer was going to carry out the instruction.

Finally, programmers could focus on the problem in hand rather than worrying about irrelevant technological details, and that is a good example of what abstraction is all about.

Abstraction by generalisation

There is a famous problem dating back more than 200 years to the old Prussian city of Königsberg. This beautiful city had seven bridges, and the inhabitants liked to stroll around the city on a Sunday afternoon, making sure to cross every bridge at least once. Nobody could figure out how to cross each bridge once and once only, or alternatively prove that this was impossible, and eventually the Mayor turned to the local mathematical genius Leonhard Euler.

The map of 18th century Königsberg

Euler's first step was to remove all irrelevant details from the map, and come up with an abstraction:

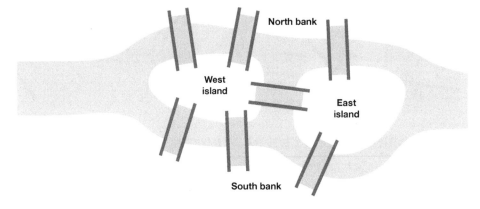

To really simplify it, Euler represented each piece of land as a circle and each bridge as a line between them.

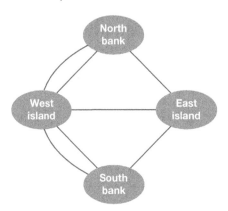

What we now have is a **graph**, with **nodes** representing land masses and **edges** (lines connecting the nodes) representing the bridges. Now that Euler had his graph, how could he solve the problem?

He did not want to try every possible solution; he realised that this was just a particular instance of a more general problem and he wanted to find a solution that was applicable to similar problems. He noticed a critical feature of the puzzle: since each bridge could be crossed only once, each node had to have an even number of connections, because you must enter and leave a node by a different edge. The only exceptions are the start and end node, since you don't have to enter a start node or leave the end node.

All the nodes in this graph have an odd number of nodes, so it is therefore impossible!

Euler had laid the foundation of graph theory, which you will come back to in the second year of this course.

By abstracting the problem, Euler made possible the solution of innumerable related problems. Not only does it apply to different cities with different numbers of bridges, it applies to many other problems with similar requirements.

Abstraction by generalisation, as illustrated above, is a grouping by common characteristics to arrive at a hierarchical relationship of the "is a kind of" type. Thus Euler's problem is a particular instance of graph theory.

This type of abstraction is very common in object-oriented programming. A class of object, say an Animal, will be defined with its own attributes such as gender and whether it is carnivore or vegetarian, and its own behaviours, methods or procedures such as move, sleep, eat, etc. Other objects such as Dog, Cat, Mouse and so on may be defined as sub-classes of Animal - they all share common characteristics which are defined in the Animal class, but have their own attributes and behaviours as well. In other words Dog "is a kind of" Animal, as are Cat and Mouse.

Q1: Use abstraction by generalisation to continue the sequence 1,4,9,16... What is the 50th number in the sequence?

2-11

Procedural abstraction

Computer science is, in broad terms, the study of problem-solving, and as such, is also the study of **abstraction**. As we have seen, abstraction allows us to separate the **physical** reality of a problem from the **logical** view. Thus, for example, you can send an email, play music or download an image without knowing any of the detail of how these things are actually done. On the other hand, the computer engineers, technicians and system administrators who enable these things to happen have a very different view. They need to be able to control the low-level details that users are not even aware of.

Procedural abstraction means using a procedure to carry out a sequence of steps for achieving some task such as calculating a student's grade from her marks in three exam papers, buying groceries online or drawing a house on a computer screen.

Consider, for example, how you could code a program to create the plan for an estate of 100 new houses. You could use a procedure which will draw a triangle of certain dimensions and colour at a particular place on the screen. The colour and dimension are passed as arguments to the procedure, for example:

```
procedure drawTriangle(colour, base, height)
```

This may be called using the statement

```
drawTriangle("red", 4.5,2.0)
```

The programmer does not need to know the details of how this procedure works. She simply needs to know how the procedure is called and what arguments are required, what data type each one is and what order they must be written in. This is called the **procedure interface**.

Similarly, there may be a procedure to build a rectangle that is defined by parameters colour, height and width, which are passed as arguments:

```
drawRectangle ("beige", 4.0, 5.0)
```

To draw a house at a given position on the screen, the programmer may write a procedure `buildHouse()` which uses the `drawTriangle()` and `drawRectangle()` procedures, aligns them and positions the house at a particular position on the screen. All these variables will be passed as arguments to the procedure.

Several houses could be combined to make a street. Several streets could be drawn to represent the estate.

Then, if the builder of the new estate decides to make all the houses larger, the procedure for drawing the house does not need to be changed - it is simply called with new arguments.

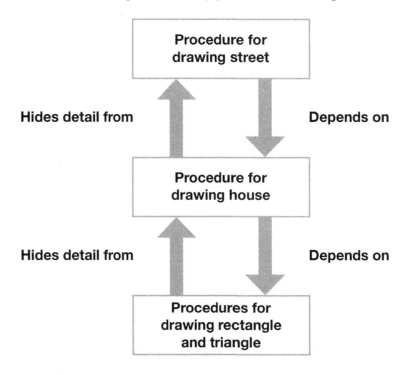

Functional abstraction

A function is called to return the result of a particular problem. For example,

```
x = sqrt(17)
```

The computation method is of no concern to the user and is hidden.

Functional abstraction, then, is a mapping from one set of values to another. The result of this mapping is unique to a given set of inputs, and a value must always be returned.

> **Q2:** List some other functions that you can call in a high level programming language without having to worry about the details of how they work.

Data abstraction

A similar idea is that of **data abstraction**.

The details of how data are actually represented are hidden. For example, when you use integers or real numbers in a program, you are not interested in how these numbers are actually represented in the computer.

In a higher level language, it is possible to create **abstract data types** such as queues, stacks and trees. The abstract data type, for example a queue, is a logical description of how the data is viewed and the operations that can be performed on it. For example, elements can be added to the rear of the queue and removed from the front. The queue may have a maximum size that cannot be exceeded. The programmer using this data structure, however, is concerned only with the operations such as `AddToQueue` or `RemoveFromQueue` and does not need to know how the data structure is implemented using, for example, an array and pointers to the front and rear of the queue.

Information hiding

Information hiding is where data is not directly accessible and can only be accessed through defined procedures/functions. This is most commonly seen in object-oriented programming, for example in a class where the data or attributes of the class are private and can only be accessed through public functions.

Decomposition and Composition

Decomposition is breaking down a complex problem into a number of sub-problems, each of which performs an identifiable task. **Composition** is the opposite – combining procedures to form compound procedures (e.g. BuildHouse, BuildStreet). It can also mean combining objects to form compound data, for example records or a data structure such as a queue, tree or list.

Problem abstraction

2-11

Problem abstraction involves removing details until the problem is represented in a way that it is possible to solve because it reduces to one that has already been solved. For example, the problem of how to find your way through a maze can be reduced to a problem of traversing a graph, for which there is an algorithm - something you will be studying in the second year of this course! (See Chapter 47 of the A Level textbook.)

Consider the following problem:

There are four knights on a 3x3 chessboard: the two white knights are at the bottom two corners, and the two black knights are at the two upper corners. The goal is to switch the knights in the minimum number of moves so that the white knights are in the upper corners and the black knights are in the bottom corners. (A knight can only move in the following manner: one or two squares horizontally or vertically, followed by two squares or one square at right angles, moving 3 squares in total.)

We can abstract this problem by first numbering the squares of the chessboard. 1 to 9. Now we can draw lines from 1 to 6 and 1 to 8 representing the two possible moves from square 1. Do the same for each square in turn, and you end up with the graph shown in (b). (Square 5 can't be reached with a knight's move so it is omitted from this graph.)

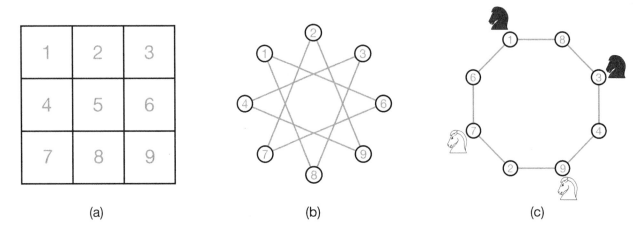

(a)   (b)   (c)

Figure (b) is not much help in solving the problem. Now imagine that all the vertices are joined by a single string, and now rearrange the string so that the vertices form a circle – this gives us a much more revealing picture. There are only two ways to solve the puzzle in the minimum number of moves; move the knights along the edges in either a clockwise or a counter-clockwise direction until each of the knights reaches the diagonally opposite corner for the first time.

This can be seen as a **'graph unfolding'** problem, equivalent to a general problem that has already been solved in the same way, so is a **reduction** of the more general problem.

Q3: What is the total number of moves required to switch the knights to the opposite side of the board?

2-11

Automation

Automation in computer science deals with building and putting into action models to solve problems. For example, you could model the financial implications of running an ice-cream stand at a given venue for a week or a longer period. You have to decide on what has to be included in the model and what assumptions you are going to make. Then you have to create and implement the algorithms and execute and test the results.

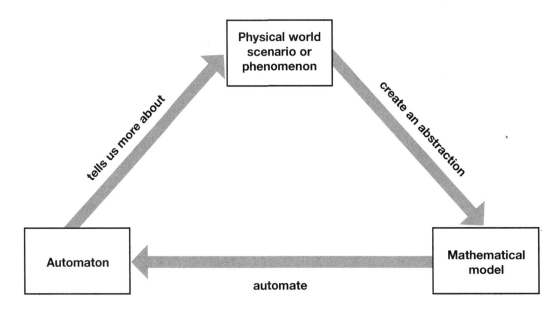

Automating the abstraction may in fact tell us more about the reality that we are modelling.

Exercises

1. "Representational abstraction is a representation arrived at by removing unnecessary details."

   Describe what this means in relation to a computer program which allows the user to enter a starting address **A** and a destination address **B** and returns a map of the route, the number of miles and the estimated journey time it will take to travel by car from **A** to **B**.   [5]

   ▼   Suggested routes

   M25   **213 mi, 3 hours 43 mins**

   ⊚ In current traffic: 3 hours 47 mins

2. Explain how **information hiding** and **procedural abstraction** could be used in a game program in which the player has to collect treasure in a cave and avoid being eaten by a monster.   [5]

3. Describe briefly **three** ways in which computer scientists make use of the concept of **abstraction** in solving problems.   [6]

4. The goal in this problem is to place as many coins as possible at points of the 8-pointed star depicted below, according to the following rules:

   - Each coin must first be placed on an unoccupied point and then moved along a line to an unoccupied point

   - Once a coin has been positioned, it cannot be moved again.

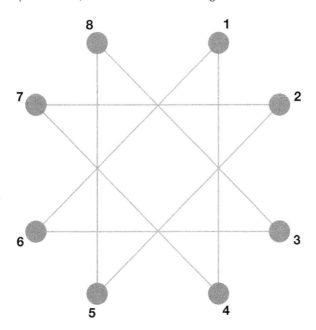

   For example, you could make the following sequence of moves: 1 → 4, 2 → 5, 3 → 6, 7 → 2, 8 → 3 which places 5 coins.

   What is the maximum number of coins that can be placed?   [1]

   Tip: Use the "graph unfolding" method of solution explained on the previous page.

Chapter 12– Finite state machines

Objectives

- Understand what is meant by a finite state machine
- List some of the uses of a finite state machine
- Draw and interpret simple state transition diagrams for finite state machines with no output
- Draw a state transition table for a finite state machine with no output and vice versa

What is a finite state machine?

A finite state machine is a model of computation used to design computer programs and sequential logic circuits. It is not a "machine" in the physical sense of a washing machine, an engine or a power tool, for example, but rather an abstract model of how a machine reacts to an external event. The machine can be in one of a finite number of states and changes from one state to the next state when triggered by some condition or input (say, a signal from a timer).

In a finite state machine:

- The machine can only be in one state at a time
- It can change from one state to another in response to an event or condition; this is called a **transition**. Often this is a switch or a binary sensor.
- The Finite State Machine (FSM) is defined by a list of its states and the condition for each transition

There can be outputs linked to the FSM's state, but in this chapter we will be considering only FSMs with no output.

Example 1

Draw an FSM to model the states and transitions of a door. The door can be open, closed or locked. It can change from the state of being open to closed, from closed to locked, but not, say, from locked to open. (It has to be unlocked first.)

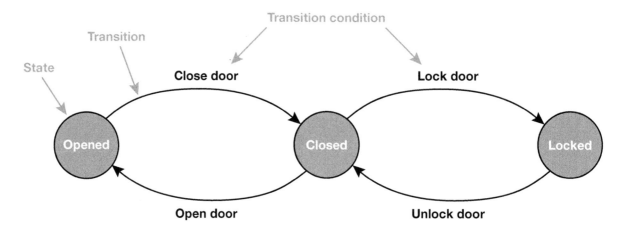

Example 2

Draw an FSM to represent a light switch. When the button is pressed, the light goes on. When the button is pressed again, the light goes off.

There is just one input B to this system: Button pressed (B=1) or Button not pressed (B=0).

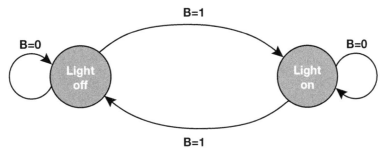

Notice that in each state, both the transitions B=0 and B=1 are drawn. If the light is off, the transition B=0 has no effect so the transition results in the same state. Likewise, if the light is on, as long as the button is not pressed, the light will stay on.

Usage of finite state machines

FSMs are widely used in modelling the design of hardware digital systems, compilers and network protocols. They are also used in the definition of languages, and to decide whether a particular word is allowed in the language.

A finite state machine which has no output is also known as a **finite state automaton**. It has a start state and a set of accept states which define whether it accepts or rejects finite strings or symbols. The finite state automaton accepts a string $c_1, c_2 \ldots c_n$ if there is a path for the given input from the start state to an accept state. The language recognised by the finite state automaton consists of all the strings accepted by it.

If, when you are in a particular state, the next state is uniquely determined by the input, it is a **deterministic final state automaton**. All the examples which follow satisfy this condition.

Notation

Symbol	Meaning
⬤	State
➔⬤	Start state
⬤ (double circle)	Accept state
⌒➔	Transition

2-12

Example 3

Use an FSM to represent a valid identifier in a programming language. The rules for a valid identifier for this particular language are:

- The identifier must start with a lowercase letter
- Any combination of letters and lowercase numbers may follow
- There is no limit on the length of the identifier

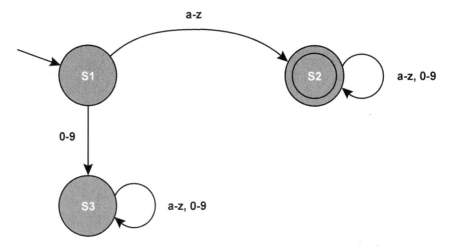

In this diagram, the **start state** S1 is represented by a circle with an arrow leading into it.

The **accept state** S2 is denoted by a double circle.

S3 is a "dead state" because having arrived here, the string can never reach the accept state.

Each character of the input string is input sequentially to the FSM and if the last character reaches the final state S2 (the **accept** state), the string is valid and is accepted. If it ends up anywhere else the string is invalid.

Note that there can only be one starting state but there may be more than one accept state (or no accept states).

Q1: Which of the following strings is valid and accepted by this finite state machine?
(i) a   (ii) bba   (iii) abbaa   (iv) bbbb

2-12

Example 4

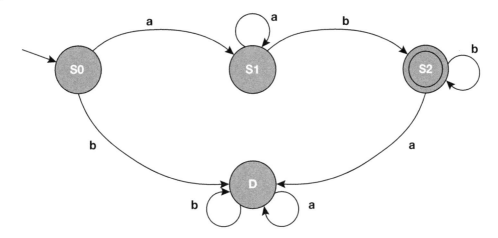

This FSM takes a string, e.g. aaabb, baa, aba. If after reading the whole string, you reach the accept state, the string is valid.

The first of these strings is accepted. What about the other two?

Q2: Can you formulate a rule for a valid string in this language?

State transition tables

An alternative representation of an FSM is a **state transition table**. This shows the current state and the next state for each input. The table below corresponds to the finite state diagram in Example 4 above.

Current state	Next state	
	Input = a	Input = b
S0	S1	D
S1	S1	S2
S2	D	S2
D	D	D

Example 5

Draw the state transition diagram and the equivalent state transition table for a language in which an empty string or a string of any length in the form *ababab* is accepted, and any other string is rejected.

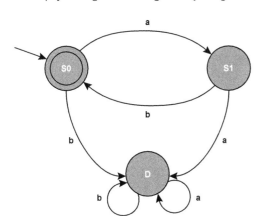

Current state	Next state	
	Input = a	Input = b
S0	S1	D
S1	D	S0
D	D	D

Exercises

1. Figure 2 shows the state transition diagram of a finite state machine (FSM) used to control a vending machine.

    The vending machine dispenses a drink when a customer has inserted exactly 50 pence.

    A transaction is cancelled and coins returned to the customer if more than 50 pence is inserted or the reject button (R) is pressed. The vending machine accepts 10, 20 and 50 pence coins. Only one type of drink is available.

    The only acceptable inputs for the FSM are 10, 20, 50 and R.

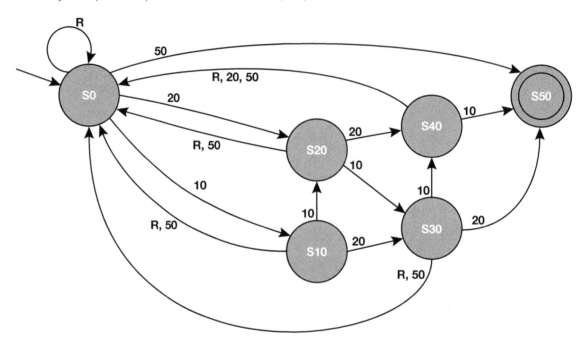

Figure 2

An FSM can be represented as a state transition diagram or as a state transition table. Table 2 is an incomplete state transition table for part of Figure 2.

(a) Complete the missing sections of the four rows of Table 2.

Original state	Input	New state
S0	10	S10
S0		
S0		
S0		

Table 2 [3]

There are different ways that a customer can provide **exactly three** inputs that will result in the vending machine dispensing a drink. Three possible permutations are "20, 10, 20", "10, R, 50" and "10, 50, 50".

(b) List **four** other possible permutations of **exactly three** inputs that will be accepted by the FSM shown in Figure 2. [4]

AQA Comp1 Qu 4 June 2012

Exercises continued

2. Figure 2 shows a Finite State Automaton (FSA). The FSA has input alphabet {0, 1} and five states, S1, S2, S3, S4 and S5.

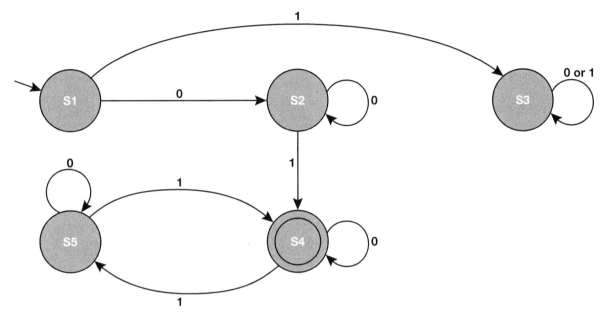

Figure 2

(a) Complete the transition table below for the FSA in Figure 2.

Current state	S_1	S_1	S_2	S_2	S_3	S_3	S_4	S_4	S_5	S_5
Input symbol	0	1	0	1	0	1				
Next state	S_2	S_3	S_2	S_4	S_3	S_3				

[1]

(b) The state S4 is a special state. This is indicated by the double circle in the diagram.

What does the double circle signify? [1]

(c) Write Yes or No in each row of the table below to indicate whether or not each of the four input strings would be accepted by the FSA in Figure 2. [2]

Input string	String accepted? (Yes/No)
101	
000	
010001101	
0100011011	

(d) Describe the language (set of strings) that the FSA will accept. [2]

AQA Comp 3 Qu 4 June 2011

2-12

Exercises continued

3. (a) A **state transition diagram** models the operation of a hotel lift. A program is written to simulate the behaviour of the lift in a hotel.

Describe **three** states that should be present in this diagram. [3]

(b) Figure 1 shows a state transition diagram for a problem which has two states S1 and S2.

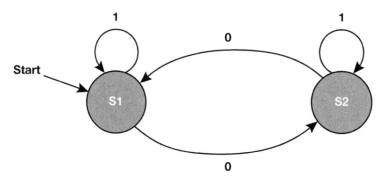

Figure 1

Table 1 is a state transition table for Figure 1. The **Next State** column is incomplete. Complete the table.

Input	Current state	Next state
0	S1	S2
0	S2	
1	S1	
1	S2	

Table 1 [3]

AQA Comp 1 Qu 3 June 2009

Section 3

Data representation

In this section:

3

Chapter 13– Number systems

Objectives

- Define a natural number, an integer and a real number
- Explain the difference between a rational and irrational number by example
- Understand and use ordinal numbers in context
- Convert between binary, decimal and hexadecimal number systems

Number types

On the number line, any whole number, for example, -10, -4, 0, 7, 1076 or 130793879 is an **integer**.

A **natural** number is a whole number that is used in counting. For example, *five gold rings*, *four* calling birds, *three* French hens. The (infinite) set of natural numbers, including zero, is referred to as $\mathbb{N}$ in mathematics. Thus $\mathbb{N}$ = {0, 1, 2, 3, …}

A **rational** number is any value that can be expressed as a ratio, or fraction. This includes all integer values since each can simply be expressed as 7/1 or 1076/1, to use the examples above.

An **irrational** number such as **pi** is one that cannot be expressed as a fraction and which has an endless series of non-repeating digits. Pi (π) can be expressed as 3.141592…. but not as a fraction. 22/7 gets close, but it's not correct. An irrational number cannot be correctly represented using a finite number of digits, and therefore a rounding error will occur.

Number	Ratio or fraction	Rational or irrational?
1.75	7/4	Rational
0.3333333 recurring	1/3	Rational
$\sqrt{2}$	Cannot be expressed as a fraction	Irrational

In mathematics, the set of integers is referred to as $\mathbb{Z}$ and the set of rational numbers is expressed as $\mathbb{Q}$. All integers are rational numbers, so $\mathbb{Z}$ = {…, -3, -2, -1, 0, 1, 2, 3, …}

A real number is any natural, rational or irrational number. The set $\mathbb{R}$ of real numbers is defined as 'the set of all possible real world quantities'. This includes, for example, -10, -6.456, 0.4, 6.0, $\sqrt{2}$ and π. It does not include 'imaginary' numbers such as $\sqrt{-1}$, or infinity (∞). In programming languages, the data type 'real' has a slightly different meaning and is defined simply as a number with a decimal point.

The set of real numbers is represented by the symbol $\mathbb{R}$. While natural numbers are used for counting, real numbers are commonly used for measurement.

Ordinal numbers

Ordinal numbers describe the numerical position of objects: *first* in a race, *second* turn on the left. They are used as pointers to a particular element in a sequence, or to define the position of something in a list; for example, an array pointer. Characters and integers are examples of ordinal data types.

Number bases

Our familiar **decimal** (or **denary**) number system uses the digits 0 through 9 and therefore has a base of 10. Binary uses only the digits 0 and 1 and has a base of 2. **Hexadecimal** uses a base of 16 with digits 0-9 and letters A to F. A number's base can be written as a subscript to denote its value in the correct number system. For example 11_{10} denotes the number eleven in decimal. 11_2 would denote a binary value, (with a decimal equivalent of three) and 11_{16} would denote a hexadecimal value. (17 in decimal.)

The binary number system

In order to better understand the simplicity of the binary number system, it is best to examine how our familiar decimal number system works. Columns, right-to-left, represent units, tens and hundreds etc. We mentally multiply the values with their column value and add the totals together.

1000s	100s	10s	1s		
5	0	7	4		
5000		+ 70	+ 4	=	**5074**

The principle is exactly the same in the binary number system. As we move from right to left, each digit is worth twice as much as the previous one, instead of ten times as much.

128	64	32	16	8	4	2	1		
1	1	0	0	1	0	1	1		
128	+ 64			+ 8		+ 2	+ 1	=	**203**

The minimum and maximum values that can be represented using unsigned binary for n bits are 0 and $2^n - 1$ respectively.

3-13

Q1: Convert the binary numbers 0011 1001 and 1111 1111 into decimal.

Converting from decimal to binary

To convert a decimal number to binary, first write headings from right to left of 1, 2, 4, 8 ... 128. (If the number given is greater than 255, continue writing headings).

To convert a number, for example 73, to binary, write a 1 under the largest heading less than 73 (i.e. 64). You now have 73 – 64 = 9 remaining, to be converted to binary. 9 = 8 + 1 so put 1 under 8 and under 1. Fill the spaces with zeros. The binary number representing 73 is 01001001.

128	64	32	16	8	4	2	1
0	1	0	0	1	0	0	1

Q2: Convert the decimal numbers 37 and 100 into binary.

The hexadecimal number system

The hexadecimal system, often referred to as simply 'hex', uses a base of 16 as follows:

Decimal	Hexadecimal	Binary
0	0	0
1	1	1
2	2	10
3	3	11
4	4	100
5	5	101
6	6	110
7	7	111
8	8	1000
9	9	1001
10	A	1010
11	B	1011
12	C	1100
13	D	1101
14	E	1110
15	F	1111
16	10	10000

Converting from binary to hexadecimal and vice versa

To convert a binary number to hexadecimal, split the binary number into groups of 4 binary digits.

Binary	0011	1010	1111	1001	
Hex	3	A	F	9	= 3AF9

To convert from hex to binary, perform this operation in reverse by grouping the bits in groups of 4 and translating each group into binary. For example, to convert the number 23_{16} to binary

Hex	2	3	
Binary	0010	0011	= 00100011

Q3: Convert the hexadecimal number A7 into binary.

Q4: What is 1111 1111 in hexadecimal?

Converting from hexadecimal to decimal and vice versa

To convert from hexadecimal to decimal, remember that the left column now represents 16s and not tens. For example, to convert 27_{16} to decimal:

	16s	1s	
Hex	2	7	$= 2 \times 16 + 7 = 39$

To convert a decimal number to hex, the easiest way is to first convert the decimal number to binary and then from binary to hex. For example, to convert 75_{10} to hex:

	128	64	32	16	8	4	2	1
Binary	0	1	0	0	1	0	1	1
Hex			4				B	

Therefore $75_{10} = 4B_{16}$ (75/16 = 4 remainder 11, or 4B, since 11 is B in hexadecimal).

3-13

Q5: Convert the decimal numbers 37 and 100 into hexadecimal.

Q6: Convert the hexadecimal numbers 3B and 14 into binary.

Why the hexadecimal number system is used

The hexadecimal system is used as a shorthand for binary since it is simple to represent a byte in just two digits, and fewer mistakes are likely to be made in writing a hex number than a string of binary digits. It is easier for technicians and computer users to write or remember a hex number than a binary number. Colour codes in images often use hexadecimal to represent the RGB values, as they are much easier to remember than a 24-bit binary string. In the example below #364DB2 represents 36_{16} for Red, $4D_{16}$ for Green and $B2_{16}$ for Blue values, which can be displayed or printed in the Colour Picker window more compactly.

Exercises

1. Represent the decimal number 123 in binary using 8 bits. [1]

2. How many different decimal numbers can be represented using 8-bit binary? [1]

3. What is the hexadecimal equivalent of the decimal number 123? [1]

4. Why are bit patterns often displayed using hexadecimal instead of binary? [2]

1	0	1	0	0	1	1	1

Figure 1

5. Figure 1 shows the contents of a memory location. What is the decimal equivalent of the contents of this memory location if it represents an unsigned binary integer? [1]

6. What is the hexadecimal equivalent of the binary pattern shown in Figure 1? [1]

7. Convert the hexadecimal number DA to decimal. [1]

8. Give **one** example of a natural number and **one** example of an irrational number. [2]

9. Which of the following, if any, are **not** part of the set $\mathbb{R}$ of real numbers?
   -12.75, 0, 22/7, 58, $\sqrt{2}$ [1]

Chapter 14 – Bits, bytes and binary

Objectives

- Define a bit as a 1 or a 0, and a byte as a group of eight bits
- Know that 2^n different values can be represented with n bits
- Use names, symbols and corresponding powers of 2 for binary prefixes e.g. Ki, Mi, Gi, Ti
- Differentiate between the character code of a decimal digit and its pure binary representation
- Describe ASCII and Unicode coding systems and explain why Unicode was introduced
- Describe methods used for error-checking and correction

Bits and bytes

A **bit** is the fundamental unit of information in the form of either a single 1 or 0. 1 and 0 are used to represent the two electronic states: on and off, or more accurately a switch that is closed (to complete a circuit) or open (to break it). A **byte** is a set of eight bits, for example 0110 1101. A set of four bits is referred to as a **nibble**.

Q1: Why is the on/off symbol designed like this:

3-14

The number of values that can be represented with n bits is 2^n. Two bits can represent 4 different values: 00, 01, 10 and 11. Three bits can represent 8 values and four bits can represent 16 different values, since 2 x 2 x 2 x 2 = 16.

Unit nomenclature

Although we frequently refer to 1024 bytes as a kilobyte, it is, in fact a **kibibyte**. To avoid any confusion between references to 1024 bytes rather than 1000 bytes, an international collaboration between standards organisations decided in 1996 that kibi would represent 1024, and kilo would represent 1000. Kibi is a combination of the words **k**ilo and **bi**nary. The same is true of the other familiar names Mega, Giga and Tera being replaced by mebi, gibi and tebi. The table below outlines the nomenclature for increasing quantities of bytes, in which a **KiB** is a **kibibyte** and a **MiB**, a **mebibyte**.

Name	Symbol	Power	Value
kibi	Ki	2^{10}	1024
mebi	Mi	2^{20}	1,048,576
gibi	Gi	2^{30}	1,073,741,824
tebi	Ti	2^{40}	1,099,511,627,776
pebi	Pi	2^{50}	1,125,899,906,842,624
exbi	Ei	2^{60}	1,152,921,504,606,846,976
zebi	Zi	2^{70}	1,180,591,620,717,411,303,424
yobi	Yi	2^{80}	1,208,925,819,614,629,174,706,176

Name	Symbol	Power
Kilo	K or k	10^3
Mega	M	10^6
Giga	G	10^9
Tera	T	10^{12}
Peta	P	10^{15}
Exa	E	10^{18}
Zetta	Z	10^{21}
Yotta	Y	10^{24}

The ASCII code

Historically, the standard code for representing the characters on the keyboard was ASCII (American Standard Code for Information Interchange). This uses seven bits which form 128 different bit combinations, more than enough to cover all of the characters on a standard English-language keyboard. The first 32 codes represent non-printing characters used for control such as **backspace** (code 8), the **Enter** or **Carriage Return** key (code 13) and the **Escape** key (code 27). The **Space** character is also included as code 32 and **Delete** as code 127.

ASCII	DEC	Binary	ASCII	DEC	Binary	ASCII	DEC	Binary	ASCII	DEC	Binary
NULL	000	000 0000	space	032	010 0000	@	064	100 0000	`	096	110 0000
SOH	001	000 0001	!	033	010 0001	A	065	100 0001	a	097	110 0001
STX	002	000 0010	"	034	010 0010	B	066	100 0010	b	098	110 0010
ETX	003	000 0011	#	035	010 0011	C	067	100 0011	c	099	110 0011
EOT	004	000 0100	$	036	010 0100	D	068	100 0100	d	100	110 0100
ENQ	005	000 0101	%	037	010 0101	E	069	100 0101	e	101	110 0101
ACK	006	000 0110	&	038	010 0110	F	070	100 0110	f	102	110 0110
BEL	007	000 0111	'	039	010 0111	G	071	100 0111	g	103	110 0111
BS	008	000 1000	(	040	010 1000	H	072	100 1000	h	104	110 1000
HT	009	000 1001	)	041	010 1001	I	073	100 1001	i	105	110 1001
LF	010	000 1010	*	042	010 1010	J	074	100 1010	j	106	110 1010
VT	011	000 1011	+	043	010 1011	K	075	100 1011	k	107	110 1011
FF	012	000 1100	,	044	010 1100	L	076	100 1100	l	108	110 1100
CR	013	000 1101	-	045	010 1101	M	077	100 1101	m	109	110 1101
SO	014	000 1110	.	046	010 1110	N	078	100 1110	n	110	110 1110
SI	015	000 1111	/	047	010 1111	O	079	100 1111	o	111	110 1111
DLE	016	001 0000	0	048	011 0000	P	080	101 0000	p	112	111 0000
DC1	017	001 0001	1	049	011 0001	Q	081	101 0001	q	113	111 0001
DC2	018	001 0010	2	050	011 0010	R	082	101 0010	r	114	111 0010
DC3	019	001 0011	3	051	011 0011	S	083	101 0011	s	115	111 0011
DC4	020	001 0100	4	052	011 0100	T	084	101 0100	t	116	111 0100
NAK	021	001 0101	5	053	011 0101	U	085	101 0101	u	117	111 0101
SYN	022	001 0110	6	054	011 0110	V	086	101 0110	v	118	111 0110
ETB	023	001 0111	7	055	011 0111	W	087	101 0111	w	119	111 0111
CAN	024	001 1000	8	056	011 1000	X	088	101 1000	x	120	111 1000
EM	025	001 1001	9	057	011 1001	Y	089	101 1001	y	121	111 1001
SUB	026	001 1010	:	058	011 1010	Z	090	101 1010	z	122	111 1010
ESC	027	001 1011	;	059	011 1011	[	091	101 1011	{	123	111 1011
FS	028	001 1100	<	060	011 1100	\	092	101 1100	|	124	111 1100
GS	029	001 1101	=	061	011 1101	]	093	101 1101	}	125	111 1101
RS	030	001 1110	>	062	011 1110	^	094	101 1110	~	126	111 1110
US	031	001 1111	?	063	011 1111	_	095	101 1111	DEL	127	111 1111

3-14

Q2: How would the word 'Cat' be stored?

Character form of a decimal digit

Although numbers are represented within the code, the number character is not the same as the actual number value. The ASCII value 0110111 will print the character '7', even though the same binary value equates to the decimal number 55. Therefore ASCII cannot be used for arithmetic and would use unnecessary space to store numbers. Numbers for arithmetic are stored as pure binary numbers.

'7' + '7' (i.e. 0110111 + 0110111 in ASCII) would be 77, not 14 or 110.

The development of ASCII

ASCII originally used only 7 bits, but an 8-bit version was developed to include an additional 128 combinations to represent symbols such as æ, © and ƒ. You can try holding down the ALT key and typing in the code number using the number pad to type one of these symbols. For example, ALT+130 will produce é, as used in *café*. The 7-bit ASCII code is compatible with the 8-bit code and simply adds a leading 0 to all binary codes.

Unicode

By the 1980s, several coding systems had been introduced all over the world that were all incompatible with one another. This created difficultly as multilingual data was being increasingly used and a new, unified format was sought. As a result, a new 16-bit code called Unicode (UTF-16) was introduced. This allowed for 65,536 different combinations and could therefore represent alphabets from dozens of languages including Latin, Greek, Arabic and Cyrillic alphabets. The first 128 codes were the same as ASCII so compatibility was retained. A further version of Unicode called UTF-32 was also developed to include just over a million characters, and this was more than enough to handle most of the characters from all languages, including Chinese and Japanese.

However, Unicode encodings take more storage space than ASCII, significantly increasing file sizes and transmission times.

Q3: Using the Unicode UTF-16 system, how much memory would be used for the word 'Mouse'?

Error checking and correction

Bits can change erroneously during transmission owing to interference. Computers use a variety of systems to verify that the data they receive is actually the same as the data that was sent.

Parity bits

A parity bit is an additional bit that is used to check that the other bits transmitted are likely to be correct. Using 7-bit ASCII with an 8-bit system meant that there was an extra bit available. This was used as a parity bit.

Computers use either odd or even parity, and the parity bit is used to ensure that the total number of 1s in each byte, including the parity bit, equals an odd or even number. For example an R is represented by 1010010 in 7-bit ASCII:

0	1	0	1	0	0	1	0

Using odd parity, the parity bit above is the most significant bit, and becomes 0 to make the total number of 1s an odd number – in this case, 3. Using even parity, the parity bit would have been set to 1.

Q4: What would be the parity bit value for 0010110 using odd parity?

Majority voting

Majority voting is a system that requires each bit to be sent three times. If a bit value is flipped erroneously during transmission over a noisy line, the recipient computer would use the majority rule and assume that the two bits that have not changed were therefore correct.

0			0			1			0			0			1			1			0		
0	0	**1**	0	0	0	1	1	**0**	0	0	0	**1**	0	0	1	1	1	1	**0**	1	0	0	0

In the example above, each bit was sent three times. 00100110 was sent as 000 000 111 000 000 111 111 000 and received as 001 000 110 000 100 111 101 000. In the 1st, 3rd, 5th and 7th bits a transmission error changed one of the bits. Since the majority (two) of the bits were 0, in the case of the 1st bit, 0 was interpreted by the recipient as the intended bit value. The recipient computer can then reassemble the correct values, i.e. 00100110, although you may have realised that the problem with this system is a tripling in the volume of data that is sent.

Q5: Assuming 010 011 110 010 000 110 111 100 is received, what value would be accepted?

Checksums (A Level only)

A checksum is a mathematical algorithm that is applied to a 'unit' or packet of data, for example a block of 256 bytes. The data in the block is used to create a checksum value which is transmitted with the block. The same algorithm is applied to the block after transmission and if the two checksums match, the transmission is deemed to have been successful. If they do not match, an error must have occurred during transmission and the block should be transmitted again.

A simple example of a checksum algorithm is to add together all of the numerical values of each byte in the block. If any bits change, it is likely, but not guaranteed, to change the checksum, and the block should be resent. In this short block of 3 bytes, the checksum would be 114, i.e. 51+43+20.

0	0	1	1	0	0	1	1	0	0	1	0	1	0	1	1	0	0	0	1	0	1	0	0
51								43								20							
114																							

Check digits

A check digit is similar to a checksum, and is an additional digit at the end of a string of other numbers designed to check for mistakes in input or transmission. Printed books and other products have a unique ISBN (International Standard Book Number) or EAN (European Article Number), a 13-digit number which includes the calculated check digit and is printed with the barcode. The first 12 digits are the unique item number, the 13th is the check digit. This can be calculated using the Modulo 10 system.

ISBN 978-0956143051

9 780956 143051

3-14

For example, the ISBN or EAN of 978095614305 has a check digit of 1. This is calculated as follows:

ISBN	9	7	8	0	9	5	6	1	4	3	0	5	1
Weight	*1*	*3*	*1*	*3*	*1*	*3*	*1*	*3*	*1*	*3*	*1*	*3*	
Multiplication	9	21	8	0	9	15	6	3	4	9	0	15	
Addition	*Add all the numbers*												99
Remainder	*Find the remainder when divided by 10*												9
Subtraction	*Subtract the result from 10*												1

The ISBN or EAN digits are given weights of 1 and 3 alternatively. Each value is multiplied by its weight. The multiplied values are added together and divided by 10 to get a remainder of 9. The remainder is subtracted from 10 to give a check digit of 1. The published check digit is read by a barcode scanner, an algorithm to check the check digit is performed and if, as in this case, the digits match, the barcode is deemed, with almost 100% accuracy, to have been read accurately. A similar system works with credit card numbers.

Q6: Use the Modulo 10 system to check the check digit on a product or book barcode.

3-14 Exercises

1. The ASCII system uses 7 bits to represent a character. The ASCII code in decimal for the numeric character '0' is 48; other numeric characters follow on from this in sequence.
   (a) Using 7 bits, what is the ASCII code for the character '2' in binary? [1]
   (b) How many different characters can be represented using ASCII? [1]

2. One character encoding scheme is Unicode. An alternative character encoding scheme is ASCII.
   (a) State one difference between Unicode and ASCII. [1]
   (b) State one advantage and one disadvantage of using ASCII rather than Unicode for representing characters. [2]

3. How many times greater is the storage capacity of a 1 terabyte hard disk drive than that of a 256 megabyte hard disk drive?
   Show each stage of your working. [2]

4. A 'majority voting' system of error checking is used to transmit data, with each bit being sent three times.
   (a) What will be the final bit pattern received by the user if the following bit pattern is transmitted? [2]

0	0	1	0	0	0	0	0	0	0	1	1	1	0	1	1	1	1	1	0	0	0	1	0

   (b) Name one disadvantage of the 'majority voting' system for transmitting data. [1]
   (c) Assuming the transmission represents a decimal number, what number does it represent? [1]

5. Explain, with the aid of an example, how an even parity system of error checking works when transmitting data. [3]

Chapter 15 – Binary arithmetic and the representation of fractions

Objectives

- Be able to add and multiply together two unsigned binary numbers

- Convert between signed binary and decimal and vice versa

- Represent positive and negative numbers in two's complement and specify the range of n bits

- Perform subtraction using two's complement

- Understand how numbers with a fractional part can be represented in binary

- Use fixed point binary form to represent a real number in a given number of bits

Binary addition

Binary addition works in a similar way to decimal addition. If two numbers added together are equal to or greater than the base value, (in the case of decimal, 10) then the 'tens' are carried. In binary, an addition that equals 2 or more results in a carry over to the next column.

In binary, the rules for addition are as follows:

1. $0 + 0 = 0$
2. $0 + 1 = 1$
3. $1 + 0 = 1$
4. $1 + 1 = 0$ Carry 1 (This is 2 in decimal or 10 in binary.)
5. $1 + 1 + 1 = 1$ Carry 1 (This is 3 in decimal or 11 in binary.)

3-15

Use the following worked example as a guide to where and how each of the rules is implemented.

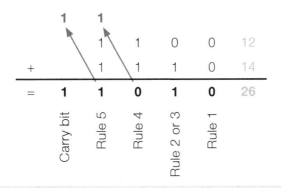

Q1: Calculate 00100111 + 00011001.

Overflow

In the following example, 8 bits are used to store the result of an addition. The result of the addition is greater than 255, and an overflow error occurs where a carry from the most significant bit requires a ninth bit.

		1	1	1				1		
		1	1	1	0	0	0	1	0	226
+		1	0	1	1	1	0	1	0	186
=	1	1	0	0	1	1	1	0	0	412

Binary multiplication

Multiplication also works in a similar way to our decimal system. In decimal, moving a number one place value to the left multiplies it by 10, and shifting it 2 places to the left multiplies it by 100.

In binary, shifting a number one place to the left multiplies it by 2. Shifting it 2 places to the left multiplies it by 4, shifting it 3 places to the left multiplies it by 8, and so on.

There are several methods of doing binary multiplication, one of them being to use a combination of shifts and addition, best shown by the example below. However, you may find the second method, using long multiplication and shown on the next page, easier to understand and apply.

For example, to multiply 22 by 2:

Answer columns

	128	64	32	16	8	4	2	1			128	64	32	16	8	4	2	1	
Multiplicand	0	0	0	1	0	1	1	0	22	Answer	0	0	1	0	1	1	0	0	44
Multiplier	0	0	0	0	0	0	1	0	2				(Multiplicand shifted left one place)						

To multiply 22 by 3, you need to add the multiplicand (multiplied by 1) to the multiplicand multiplied by 2.

Answer columns

	128	64	32	16	8	4	2	1			128	64	32	16	8	4	2	1	
Multiplicand	0	0	0	1	0	1	1	0	22		0	0	0	1	0	1	1	0	22
Multiplier	0	0	0	0	0	0	1	1	3	+	0	0	1	0	1	1	0	0	44
										Answer	0	1	0	0	0	0	1	0	66

To multiply 22 by 10, add the multiplicand multiplied by 2 to the multiplicand multiplied by 8

Answer columns

	128	64	32	16	8	4	2	1			128	64	32	16	8	4	2	1	
Multiplicand	0	0	0	1	0	1	1	0	22		0	0	1	0	1	1	0	0	44
Multiplier	0	0	0	0	1	0	1	0	10	+	1	0	1	1	0	0	0	0	176
										Answer	1	1	0	1	1	1	0	0	220

This is effectively exactly the same as performing a long multiplication sum. Compare a long multiplication in decimal with one in binary:

Decimal	Binary	
3101	10010	18
x 102	x 101	x 5
6202	10010	18
+ 0000	+ 00000	+ 0
+ 3101	+ 10010	+72
316302	1011010	90 Answer

Q2: Calculate 10111 x 1001.

Signed and unsigned binary numbers

An **unsigned** representation of a binary number can only represent positive numbers. A **signed** representation can represent both positive and negative numbers. Two's complement, described below, is one representation of a signed binary number.

Two's complement

Two's complement binary works in a similar way to numbers on an analogue counter. Moving the wheel forwards one, will create a reading of 0001; turn back one, and the reading will become 9999. 9999 is interpreted as -1.

3-15

In binary:

11111101	=	-3
11111110	=	-2
11111111	=	-1
00000000	=	0
00000001	=	1
00000010	=	2
00000011	=	3

Calculating the range

The range that can be represented with two's complement using n bits is given by the formula:

$$-(2^{(n-1)}) \ldots 2^{(n-1)} - 1$$

With eight bits, the maximum decimal range that can be represented is -128 to 127 because the leftmost bit is used as a sign bit to indicate whether a number is negative. If the leftmost number is a 1, it is a negative number. Thus 10000000 represents -128

Q3: What is the range that can be represented using 16 bits?

Converting a negative decimal number to binary

Start by working out the positive equivalent of the number, flip all of the bits and add 1. For example, to convert the decimal number -9 to binary:

		-9
Positive binary	:	00001001
Flip the bits	:	11110110
Add one	:	1
		11110111

Converting a negative two's complement binary number to decimal

The same method works the other way. Flip all of the bits and add 1. Then work out the result in decimal using the normal method. For example, to convert the binary number 11100101 to decimal:

		11100101
Flip the bits	:	00011010
Add one	:	1
Convert	:	-00011011
		-27

Binary subtraction using two's complement

Binary subtraction is best done by using the negative two's complement number and then adding the second number. For example decimal 17-14 would be:

14	=	00001110
-14	=	11110010
17	=	00010001
17 + (-14)	=	(1)00000011

The carry on the addition is ignored, and the correct answer is given.

Fixed point binary numbers

Fixed point binary numbers can be a useful way to represent fractions in binary. A binary point is used to separate the whole place values from the fractional part on the number line:

In the binary example above, the left hand section before the point is equal to 5 (4+1) and the right hand section is equal to ½ + ¼ (¾), or 0.5 + 0.25 = 0.75. So, using four bits after the point, 0101 1100 is 5.75 in decimal. A useful table with some decimal fractions and their equivalents is given below:

Q4: How is 19.25 represented using a single byte with 3 bits after the point?

Binary fraction	Fraction	Decimal fraction
0.1	1/2	0.5
0.01	1/4	0.25
0.001	1/8	0.125
0.0001	1/16	0.0625
0.00001	1/32	0.03125
0.000001	1/64	0.015625
0.0000001	1/128	0.0078125
0.00000001	1/256	0.00390625

Converting a decimal fraction to fixed point binary

To convert the fractional part of a decimal to binary, you can employ the same technique as you would when converting any decimal number to binary. Take the value and subtract each point value from the amount until you are left with 0. Take the example 3.5625 using 4 bits to the right of the binary point:

Subtract 0.5:	0.5625 – 0.5 = 0.0625	**1**
Subtract 0.25 from 0.0625:	Won't go	**0**
Subtract 0.125 from 0.0625:	Won't go	**0**
Subtract 0.0625 from 0.0625:	0.0625 – 0.0625 = 0	**1**

3 = 0011 in binary. 0.5625 = 1001. So 3.5625 = 0011 1001

It is worth noticing that in this system, some fractions cannot be represented at all. 0.2, 0.3 and 0.4, for example, will require an infinite number of bits to the right of the point. The number of fractional places would therefore be truncated and the number will not be accurately stored, causing rounding errors. In our decimal system, two decimal places can hold all values between .00 and .99. With the fixed point binary system, 2 digits after the point can only represent 0, ¼, ½, or ¾ and nothing in between.

The range of a fixed point binary number is also limited by the fractional part. For example, if you have only 8 bits to store a number to 2 binary places, you would need 2 digits after the point, leaving only 6 bits before it. 6 bits only gives a range of 0-63. Moving the point one to the left to improve accuracy within the fractional part also serves to half the range to just 0-31. Even with 32 bits used for each number, including 8 bits for the fractional part after the point, the maximum value is only about 8 million. Another format called floating point binary may be used, but this is not examined at AS Level.

3-15

Exercises

1. Represent the decimal value -19 as an 8-bit two's complement binary integer. [2]

2. What is the largest positive decimal value that can be represented using 8-bit two's complement binary? [1]

3. Describe how 8-bit two's complement binary can be used to subtract one number from another number. In your answer show how the calculation 25 – 49 would be completed using the method that you have described. [2]

4. A computer stores the current temperature of a supermarket delivery van.
    The temperature in °C is stored as a two's complement integer using a single byte.

    (a) Convert the freezer temperature value of -19 into binary. [2]

    (b) State the range of temperature values that can be stored using 8 bits. [1]

5. A memory location contains the value 10101011. What is its decimal equivalent if it represents a two's complement binary integer? [2]

6. Using 1 byte to hold each number, with an imaginary binary point fixed after the fourth digit, convert the following decimal numbers to binary:

    (a) (i) 4.25   (ii) 7.1875   (iii) 6.875 [3]

    (b) Convert the following binary numbers to decimal, assuming four bits after the point:
        (i) 0000000001101000   (ii) 0000000000110010 [2]

    (c) What are the largest and smallest positive numbers that can be stored in two bytes assuming four bits after the binary point? [2]

Chapter 16 – Bitmapped graphics

Objectives

- Understand how bitmapped images are represented in terms of size in pixels, resolution and colour depth

- Be able to calculate storage requirements for a bitmap image

- Be aware that images contain metadata and be able to describe typical metadata

Representation of bitmapped images

A bitmap (or **raster**) image contains many picture elements or pixels, that make up the whole image. A pixel is the smallest identifiable area of an image. Each pixel is attributed a binary value which represents a single colour.

Resolution

The resolution of an image can be expressed as the **width in pixels x height in pixels**. This does not determine the size of the image, simply the number of pixels within it. Assuming an image's physical dimensions remain the same, then the greater the number of pixels it contains, the sharper the image, as the pixels must become smaller to fit inside its boundaries.

100 x 67 pixels   *1000 x 670 pixels*

Sometimes resolution is expressed as the number of pixels per inch or **PPI**. This indicates the density of the pixels, rather than the actual image dimensions. 72PPI is a standard screen resolution, and images with a resolution greater than this will not appear any better on screen. Print quality requires images at 300PPI to print in photographic quality. DPI (or Dots Per Inch) is a printing term relating to the number of ink dots per inch on a page and is often confused with PPI.

Some newer screens, including smartphones, can have a screen resolution of up to 400PPI. This makes pixels so small that they can no longer be easily distinguished by the human eye without the aid of a microscope.

Colour depth

Each pixel in an image has a binary value attributed to it. The number of bits determines the number of combinations (as n bits gives 2^n combinations), and this determines the number of colours that a pixel can represent. Each binary value represents a single colour, and the number of bits per pixel is referred to as the **colour depth**.

3-16

A simple black and white image will only require one bit per pixel, 0 to represent black and 1 to represent white.

1	1	1	0	1	1	1
1	0	1	0	1	0	1
1	1	0	0	0	1	1
0	0	0	0	0	0	0
1	1	0	0	0	1	1
1	0	1	0	1	0	1
1	1	1	0	1	1	1

This icon image has a resolution of 7x7 pixels, with 49 pixels in total. If each pixel is represented by one bit, the total image file size (ignoring metadata) will be 49 bits.

Once we begin to introduce colour, or increase the number of colours in the image, the number of bits that each pixel will need must be increased to allow for a greater number of combinations.

11	11	11	01	11	11	11
11	10	11	01	11	10	11
11	11	10	01	10	11	11
01	01	01	00	01	01	01
11	11	10	01	10	11	11
11	10	11	01	11	10	11
11	11	11	01	11	11	11

This image, although identical in size, has four colours, and will therefore require two bits per pixel to offer four combinations. The file size (ignoring metadata) will therefore double to 98 bits, with 2 bits x 49 pixels.

One byte per pixel will offer 256 different colours, 16 bits will give 65,536 colours and 24 bits will allow for over 16 million colours – approaching the number that the human eye can detect. This has become the current standard with 256 colour values (8 bits) per channel: red, green and blue. Where 32 bits are used, the last 8 bits are either ignored or used for an alpha channel to control transparency.

Q1: Given an image with a resolution of 1024 x 1024, what would the file size be if 256 colours are to be represented?

Metadata

Metadata is best described as data about data. In the case of image metadata, details such as the image **width in pixels**, **height in pixels** and **colour depth**.

The storage of this additional data with the file helps to explain why your calculated image size may not equal exactly what the computer shows as the image size. Another reason is compression which can dramatically reduce the size of an image.

Vector graphics (A Level only)

Vector graphics are represented quite differently. Rather than storing information on each individual pixel and building an image from them, vector images are made up of **geometric shapes** or **objects** such as lines, curves, arcs and polygons. A vector file stores only the necessary details about each shape in order to redraw the object when the file loads.

> **Q2:** In order to draw a square exactly as someone else intended, what information would you need to know?

3-16

To recreate an image of a circle, a computer must store its **properties**, including the **position** of its centre within the image, its **radius**, **fill** colour, **line colour** and **line weight**.

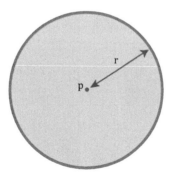

Vector drawing lists

These properties are stored in a **drawing list** which specifies how to redraw the image. If the image is resized on screen, the computer will adjust the position and dimensions of the image properties and redraw the image perfectly every time. A bitmapped image will pixelate.

The drawing list item for the circle above might appear in a drawing list like this:

Vector drawing list
Circle (centre = x,y, radius = r, fill = blue, stroke = red, weight = 3px)
Rectangle (position = x,y, width = 20, height = 60, fill = yellow, stroke = none)
Line (start = x,y, end = x,y, stroke = green, weight = 1px)

Regardless of how large these shapes are drawn, the image will always be sharp, and the amount of data required to store the image will not change.

Vector graphics versus bitmapped graphics

A **vector** image usually has a much smaller file size and will scale perfectly, regardless of how large or small you make it. A logo is often best created as a vector graphic since the company is then able to print it crisply on anything from a business card to a billboard.

**3.3KB
Bitmap**

**1.9KB
Vector**

Since they are often smaller files, vectors use less memory and storage space, transmit faster and often load more quickly. Why then, are bitmap images used at all? A vector image cannot easily replicate an image with continuous areas of changing colour such as a photograph, taken with a digital camera. Take this image below, with a vectorised equivalent. Theoretically, if you created a vector image with squares of solid colour, each 1 pixel in size, you would be able to replicate a bitmap exactly; but your file would need to store a single list item for each pixel – far more than a short binary value. Note the difference in file size and quality here:

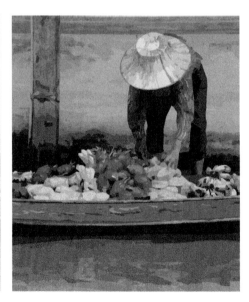

84KB – Original bitmap   *1.2MB – Vectorised version*

Individual pixels can be manipulated within a bitmap image – useful in the case of photo retouching, for example. With a vector image, individual objects are easily manipulated, but individual pixels cannot be changed.

Exercises

1. Images are often represented in a computer's main memory using bitmapped graphics. Bitmapped images consist of **pixels**. A pixel is the smallest addressable part of an image.

   (a) What is meant by the **resolution** of a bitmapped graphic image? [2]

   (b) What is meant by the **colour depth** of a bitmapped graphic image? [2]

   An image has 10 x 10 pixels. It is stored in an image format that is limited to 16 colours.

   (c) Calculate the image size in bytes. [2]

   Instead of using bitmapped graphics, images may be represented in a computer's main memory using vector graphics.

   (d) State **one** advantage of vector graphics compared with bitmapped graphics. [1]

   AQA Comp 1 Qu 3 June 2011

2. A bitmapped image consists of pixels. The figure below shows a bitmapped representation of an image of a winking, happy face consisting of red, blue, black and white pixels only.

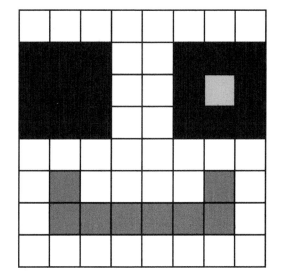

   (a) Why must at least two bits be used to represent each pixel? [1]

   The second line of pixels (from the top) has been represented in a computer's memory as the bit pattern 1111 1100 0011 1111. A black pixel is coded as 11.

   (b) Suggest a suitable 16-bit bit pattern that could be used to represent the third row of pixels. [2]

   (c) What, in bytes, is the minimum file size for the bitmapped image? [3]

   Instead of representing the face as a bitmapped image, vector graphics could have been used.

   (d) State **three** items of data that would need to be stored about an eye object, similar to those shown in the image in the above figure, if it is to be represented using vector graphics. [3]

   (e) Describe **two** advantages of using vector graphics instead of bitmaps to represent an image. [2]

   AQA Comp 1 Qu 5 June 2012

Chapter 17 – Digital representation of sound

Objectives

- Describe the digital representation of sound in terms of sampling rate and resolution
- Describe the principles of operation of an analogue to digital converter and a digital to analogue converter
- Understand and apply the Nyquist theorem
- Calculate sound sample sizes in bytes
- Describe the purpose of MIDI and the use of event messages
- Describe the advantages of using MIDI files for representing music

Sound sampling and resolution

Sound waves are naturally in a continuous, analogue form. To represent sound in a computer, the (**continuous**) analogue sound waves have to be converted to a (**discrete**) digital format. This can be done by measuring and recording the amplitude of the sound wave at given time intervals (several thousand times per second). The more frequently the samples are taken, the more accurately the sound will be represented. The frequency at which samples are taken is measured in **hertz (Hz)**, a unit of frequency equal to one cycle per second.

In addition, in the same way that an image's quality is improved with a more precise representation of colour enabled by a greater colour depth, the accuracy of a sound recording increases with a greater audio bit depth. Increasing the number of points of amplitude (represented on the y axis below) increases the accuracy at which you can record a sound's amplitude (or wave height) at a given point in time.

Q1: Which of the graphs above represents a more accurate recording? Why?

Sample rate

The **sampling rate** is the frequency with which you record the amplitude of the sound. The more often you take a sample, the smoother the playback will sound. The disadvantage of this, is that every time you take a sample, at a resolution of say 16 bits, you need to store another 2 bytes of data. A typical CD recording is made at 44,100Hz, or 44,100 times per second. This means that for every second of sound, 2 bytes x 44,100 = 88,200 / 1000 = 88.2KB is required and for every minute, approximately 5.3MB is required. For stereo sound, this is doubled to provide samples for left and right channels.

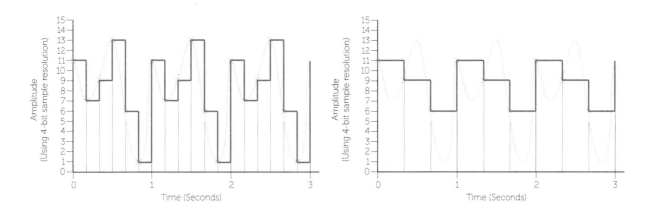

Calculating sound sample sizes

To calculate the byte size of a sample, you must multiply:

*the number of samples per second **x** the number of bits per sample **x** the length of the sample in seconds*

A sample of one minute taken at a resolution of 16 bits at 20KHz would be calculated as follows:

*20,000 **x** 16 x 60 = 19,200,000 bits **or** 2,400,000 bytes **or** 2.4MB*

If the sample is recorded in stereo, a sample for each channel is taken and therefore the sample size will double.

3-17

Q3: Calculate the kbit/s of a radio jingle recorded in stereo at 10KHz using 8 bits per sample.

Analogue and digital signals and data

The differences are shown in the table below.

	Analogue	**Digital**
Signal	A continuous signal which represents physical measurements	Discrete time signals generated by digital modulation
Representation	Uses a continuous range of values to represent information	Uses discrete or discontinuous values to represent information
Example	Human voice, mercury thermometer, tape recorder, analogue watch	Computers, CDs, DVDs, digital watch
Data	In analogue technology, a wave is recorded in its original form; for example, a signal from a microphone can be copied onto a tape, then read, amplified and sent to a speaker to produce the sound	In digital technology, analogue waveforms are sampled at intervals, turned into a limited set of numbers and stored on a digital device
Quantifying	Continuously varying quantities are measured	Quantities are counted rather than measured.

Analogue to digital conversion

During the process of converting an **analogue** sound into a **digital** recording, a microphone converts the sound energy into electrical energy. The analogue to digital converter (ADC) samples the analogue data at a given frequency, measuring the amplitude of the wave at each point and converting it into a binary value according to the resolution or audio bit depth being used for each sample.

To output a sound, the binary values for each sample point are translated back into analogue signals or voltage levels and sent to an amplifier connected to a speaker.

ADCs are used with analogue sensors such as a microphone and the most common use for a DAC is to convert a digital audio signal to an analogue signal.

Interpreting frequency

The **frequency** of a sound is determined by the speed of oscillation or vibration of a wave. This controls the pitch and is measured in **Hertz**, (Hz). By looking at a simple graph, you can interpret the frequency or pitch of the sound.

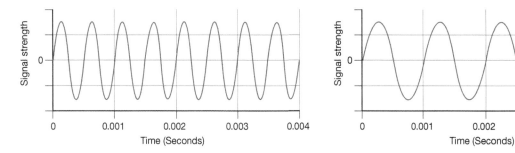

In the first example above, the wave is oscillating (from peak to trough) twice every 0.001 seconds. That equates to 2,000 oscillations per second, and would therefore have a frequency of 2,000 Hz or 2KHz. The second example would be a lower pitched sound with a frequency of 1KHz.

Nyquist's theorem

Harry **Nyquist** discovered in 1928 that in order to produce an accurate recording, the sampling rate must be at least double that of the highest frequency in the original signal. His theory was later proven in 1949 by Claude Shannon.

This means that a sound with a frequency of 10,000Hz must be sampled at a minimum of 20,000Hz in order to accurately reproduce the original. The human ear can hear frequencies between approximately 20Hz and 20,000Hz and some individuals are able to hear frequencies a little beyond that. For that reason, CDs are sampled at 44,100Hz in order for recorded sound to be reproduced accurately enough for there to be no audible distinction from the original – at least to most of us. What your dog might make of hearing a CD versus the original is another matter!

Q4: A sample is played with a maximum frequency of 12KHz. What is the minimum sampling rate that must be used when recording this sample in order to accurately replicate the sound?

3-17

Musical Instrument Digital Interface (MIDI)

MIDI is a technical standard that describes a protocol, digital interface and connectors which can be used to allow a wide variety of electronic musical instruments, computers and other related devices to connect and communicate with one another. A midi **controller** carries **event messages** that specify pitch and duration of a note, timbre, vibrato and volume changes, and synchronize tempo between multiple devices.

The ability to specify an instrument for a note makes it possible for a computer and only a few skilled musicians with a synthesiser to recreate the music of a much larger ensemble.

A **MIDI** file is not a recording of a live source. It is a list of instructions that tell it to **synthesise** a sound based on pre-recorded digital samples and synthesised samples of sounds created by different sources of instruments. A MIDI file can use 1,000 times **less disk space** than a conventional recording at an equivalent quality. The music created is also easily manipulated and the 'instructions' to play a specific song can also be passed on to other digital instruments or played in a different key

Exercises

1. To record sound a computer needs to convert the analogue sound signal into a digital form. During this process samples of the analogue signal are taken. Figure 1 shows part (0.02 seconds) of an analogue sound wave.

Figure 1

The frequency of an analogue sound wave is determined by how many waves of oscillation occur per second and is measured in Hertz (Hz) – the number of waves of oscillation per second.

(a) If the part of the analogue sound shown in Figure 1 is the highest frequency in the entire sound to be sampled, what is the minimum sampling rate (in Hz) that should be used? [2]

(b) Describe clearly the steps taken by an ADC (analogue-to-digital converter) in the conversion of an analogue sound wave to an equivalent digital signal. [3]

MIDI is an alternative method for storing sound digitally that does not use sound waves; instead, information about each musical note is stored.

(c) State one advantage of using the MIDI representation for storing sound digitally. [1]

(d) State an item of data, other than the note itself, that might be stored about a musical note in a MIDI file. [1]

AQA Comp 1 Qu 3 June 2012

Exercises continued

2. A performance by a music band is to be recorded and distributed on CD.

The figure below shows three samples stored in a computer's memory that have been taken from an analogue signal as part of the recording process. A sampling rate of 44,000Hz (Hertz) has been used.

1Hz is one sample per second.

0000 0001 1000 1110
0000 0001 1000 1110
0000 0001 1000 0011

(a) What sampling resolution has been used? [1]

(b) If the original analogue signal lasts 100 seconds, how many bytes of storage will be required to store all the samples taken in the recording process? [3]

The average human can hear frequencies up to 20,000Hz (Hertz).

(c) Explain why a sampling rate of 44,000Hz has been chosen for the recording. [2]

The CD recording is processed to create a version of the performance that can be downloaded from the band's website. The sound quality of the version of the recording stored on the web server is not as good as the sound quality of the CD version.

(d) State one possible cause of this reduction in sound quality. [1]

AQA Comp 1 Qu 3 June 2013

3. To record sound a computer needs to convert the analogue sound into a digital form. During this process samples of the sound have to be taken. Figure 2 shows 6 samples that have been stored in a computer's memory. These samples have been taken from the analogue signal over a period of one hundredth of a second.

Sample 6	01101100
Sample 5	01101100
Sample 4	01100000
Sample 3	00001101
Sample 2	00001000
Sample 1	00011011

Figure 2

Look at the digital representation, shown in Figure 2, of the analogue sound.

One Hertz (Hz) is one sample per second.

(a) What sampling rate, in Hertz, has been used? [2]

(b) What sampling resolution has been used? [1]

(c) State Nyquist's theorem. [2]

AQA Comp 1 Qu 3 June 2010

3-17

Chapter 18 – Data compression and encryption algorithms

Objectives

- Know why sound and images are often compressed

- Understand how other files can be compressed

- Understand the difference between lossless and lossy compression

- Explain the advantages and disadvantages of different compression techniques

- Explain run length encoding and dictionary based compression

- Define encryption by use of examples

- Be able to encrypt and decrypt a message using the Caesar cipher

- Understand the flaws of the Caesar cipher with reference to substitution and brute force methods

- Explain the function of the Vernam cipher by example

- Explain why the Vernam cipher is considered to have perfect security

- Compare the Vernam cipher with others that depend on computational security

Why use compression?

File compression techniques were developed to reduce the storage space of files on disk. With disk storage becoming larger and cheaper, this is less important these days, but the reduction of file size has become even more important in the sharing and transmission of data. Internet Service Providers (ISPs) and mobile phone networks impose limits and charges on bandwidth. Images on websites need to be in a compressed format to enable a web page to load quickly – even on a fast connection, music and video streaming must take advantage of compression in order to reduce buffering. (In streaming audio or video from the Internet, buffering refers to downloading a certain amount of data to a temporary storage area or buffer, before starting to play a section of the music or movie.)

Compression can be either **lossy**, where unnecessary information is removed from the original file, or **lossless**. Lossless compression retains all information required to replicate the original file exactly.

Lossy compression

Lossy compression works by removing non-essential information. The two **JPG** images overleaf are clearly identifiable as the same thing, but one has been heavily compressed, displaying untidy and blocky compression artefacts as a consequence. Nevertheless, we can make out the subject of the image well, but the degree to which they are compressed comes at the cost of quality.

Original image 310KB   *Heavily compressed image 5.7KB*

The compression of sound and video works in a similar way. **MP3** files use lossy compression to remove frequencies too high for most of us to hear and to remove quieter sounds that are played at the same time as louder sounds. The resulting file is about 10% of original size, meaning that 1 minute of MP3 audio equates to roughly 1MB in size.

Voice is transmitted over the Internet or mobile telephone networks using lossy compression and although we have no problem in understanding what the other person is saying, we can recognise the difference in quality of a voice over a phone rather than in person. The apparent difference is lost data.

3-18

Lossless compression

Lossless compression works by recording patterns in data rather than the actual data. Using these patterns and a set of instructions on how to use them, the computer can reverse the procedure and reassemble an image, sound or text file with exact accuracy and no data is lost. This is most important with the compression of program files for example, where a single lost character would result in an error in the programming code. A pixel with a slightly different colour would not be of huge consequence in most cases. Lossless compression usually results in a much larger file than a lossy file, but one that is still significantly smaller than the original.

> **Q1:** What type of compression is likely to be used for the following: a website image, a zipped file of long text documents and images, an instruction manual in PDF format?

Run Length Encoding (RLE)

If you were ordering food from a takeaway restaurant for a group of five friends, it is likely that you might ask for "5 pizzas" rather than "one pizza, and another pizza, and another pizza etc." **Run Length Encoding** exploits the same principle. Rather than recording every pixel in an image, for example, it records its value and the number of times it repeats.

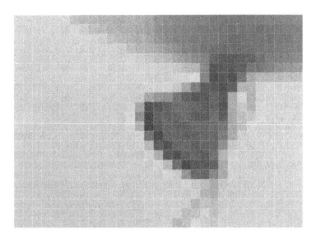

For this section of the balloon image, the encoding for the first row might crudely translate to: 6 green, 8 yellow and 17 orange, using one binary value for the colour value and another for the number of contiguous matching pixels in the run. This would reduce the data necessary to store this row to 6 bytes (00000110 00000001 00001000 00000010 00010001 00000011) rather than 31 bytes assuming a bit depth of 8 and values for each colour of 00000001, 00000010 and 00000011.

6 ■ 8 ■ 17 ■

Dictionary-based compression techniques

Suppose that instead of sending a complete message, a copy of the Oxford English Dictionary was sent alongside a coded message using the page number and the position of the word on that page. The word 'pelican' falls on page 249 as the 7th word on that page. This could be send as 249,7 – using only 2 bytes; considerably fewer than the 7 bytes it would take to send the complete word. (Ignore, for now, the additional space that it would take to send the dictionary with it!)

Dictionary based compression works in a similar way. The compression algorithm searches through the text to find suitable entries in its own dictionary (or it may use a known dictionary) and translates the message accordingly.

Number	Entry	Binary
1	Do	000
2	_unto	001
3	_others	010
4	_as	011
5	_you	100
6	_would	101
7	_have	110
8	_do	111

Using the dictionary table above, the saying **"Do unto others as you would have others do unto you"** would be compressed as **1 2 3 4 5 6 7 3 8 2 5** or in binary using only **33 bits**. This compares to 51 characters or 51 bytes – a reduction of 92%. This still ignores the fact that the dictionary must also be stored with the text, but with a longer body of text to be compressed, a dictionary becomes quite insignificant in size compared with the original, and the original message can still be reassembled perfectly.

3-18

What is encryption?

Encryption is the transformation of data from one form to another to prevent an unauthorised third party from being able to understand it. The original data or message is known as **plaintext**. The encrypted data is known as **ciphertext**. The encryption method or algorithm is known as the **cipher**, and the secret information to lock or unlock the message is known as a **key**.

The Caesar cipher and the Vernam cipher offer polar opposite examples of security. Where the Vernam offers perfect security, the Caesar cipher is very easy to break with little or no computational power. There are many others methods of encryption – some of which may take many computers, many years to break, but these are still breakable and the principles behind them are similar.

The Caesar cipher

Julius Caesar is said to have used this method to keep messages secure. The **Caesar cipher** (also known as a **shift cipher**) is a type of **substitution cipher** and works by shifting the letters of the alphabet along by a given number of characters; this parameter being the key. Below is an example of a shift cipher using a key of 5. (An algorithm for this cipher is given as an example on page 46.)

A	B	C	D	E	F	G	H	I	J	K	L	M	N	O	P	Q	R	S	T	U	V	W	X	Y	Z
↓	↓	↓	↓	↓	↓	↓	↓	↓	↓	↓	↓	↓	↓	↓	↓	↓	↓	↓	↓	↓	↓	↓	↓	↓	↓
F	G	H	I	J	K	L	M	N	O	P	Q	R	S	T	U	V	W	X	Y	Z	A	B	C	D	E

3-18

Q2: Using the table above, what is the ciphertext for 'JULIUS CAESAR' using a shift of 5?

Q3: What word can be translated from the following ciphertext, which uses a key of −2: ZYBECP

You will no doubt be able to see the ease with which you might be able to decrypt a message using this system.

DGYDQFH WR ERUGHU DQG DWWDFN DW GDZQ

Even if you had to attempt a brute force attack on the message above, there are only 25 different possibilities (since a shift of zero means the plaintext and the ciphertext are identical). Otherwise you might begin by guessing the likelihood of certain characters first and go from there. Using cryptanalysis on longer messages, you would quickly find the most common ciphertext letter and could start by assuming this was an E, for example, or perhaps an A. *(Hint.)*

Cryptanalysis and perfect security

Other ciphers that use non-random keys are open to a cryptanalytic attack and can be solved given enough time and resources. Even ciphers that use a computer-generated random key can be broken since mathematically generated random numbers are not actually random; they just appear to be so. A truly random sequence must be collected from a physical and unpredictable phenomenon such as white noise, the timing of a hard disk read/write head or radioactive decay. A truly random key must be used with a Vernam cipher to ensure it is mathematically impossible to break.

The Vernam cipher

The **Vernam cipher**, invented in 1917 by the scientist Gilbert Vernam, is one implementation of a class of ciphers known as **one-time pad ciphers**, all of which offer perfect security if used properly. All others are based on **computational security** and are theoretically discoverable given enough time, ciphertext and computational power. Frequency analysis is a common technique used to break a cipher.

One-time pad

To provide perfect security, the encryption key or **one-time pad** must be equal to or longer in characters than the plaintext, be truly random and be used only once. The sender and recipient must meet in person to securely share the key and destroy it after encryption or decryption. Since the key is random, so will be the distribution of the characters meaning that no amount of cryptanalysis will produce meaningful results.

The bitwise exclusive or XOR

A Boolean XOR operation is carried out between the binary representation of each character of the plaintext and the corresponding character of the one-time pad. The XOR operation is covered in Chapter 23 and you may want to refer to this to verify the output for any combination of 0 and 1. Use the ASCII chart on page 73 for reference.

Plaintext: M	Key: +	XOR: f
1	0	1
0	1	1
0	0	0
1	1	0
1	0	1
0	1	1
1	1	0

Q4: Using the ASCII chart and the XOR operator, what ciphertext character will be produced from the letter E with the key w?

Using this method, the message "**Meet on the bridge at 0300 hours**" encrypted using a one-time pad of **+tkiGeMxGvnhoQ0xQDlllVdT4slJm9qf** will produce the ciphertext:

$$\text{f◀♬g\#X3♂H\#Y6!i(=vTg⌐Ci"¬L⌐⌐}$$

The encryption process will often produce strange symbols or unprintable ASCII characters as in the above example, but in practice it is not necessary to translate the encrypted code back into character form, as it is transmitted in binary. To decrypt the message, the XOR operation is carried out on the ciphertext using the same one-time pad, which restores it to plaintext.

Exercises

1. Explain the difference between lossy and lossless data compression. [2]

2. Run-length encoding (RLE) is a pattern substitution compression algorithm.
   Data is stored in the format (colour,run) where 0 = White, 1 = Black.

   ```
   (0,1),(1,5),(0,1),
   (1,7),
   (1,1),(0,2),(1,1),(0,2),(1,1),
   (1,7),
   (0,1),(1,1),(0,1),(1,1),(0,1),(1,1),(0,1),
   (0,1),(1,1),(0,1),(1,1),(0,1),(1,1),(0,1),
   (0,1),(1,1),(0,3),(1,1),(0,1)
   ```

3-18

Exercises continued

(a) Reassemble the encoded sequence above to form a 7x7 web icon image in the grid below.

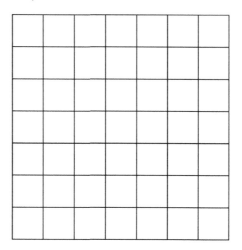

[3]

(b) RLE encoding is a lossless compression method. Give one disadvantage of lossless compression over lossy methods for the compression of images. [1]

(c) Explain why compression is considered necessary for images on the web. [2]

3. a) Explain why lossy compression techniques would not be suitable for use with files containing large bodies of text. [1]

(b) Suggest a suitable lossless method for compressing text. [1]

4. The Vernam cipher uses a one-time pad.

(a) Explain what is meant by a one-time pad. [1]

(b) Using the section of ASCII code below, apply the one-time pad **£]FL** to the word **exam** to encrypt it using the Vernam method. [4]

ASCII	DEC	Binary	ASCII	DEC	Binary	ASCII	DEC	Binary
space	032	010 0000	E	069	100 0101	`	096	110 0000
!	033	010 0001	F	070	100 0110	a	097	110 0001
"	034	010 0010	G	071	100 0111	b	098	110 0010
£	035	010 0011	K	075	100 1011	c	099	110 0011
$	036	010 0100	L	076	100 1100	d	100	110 0100
%	037	010 0101	M	077	100 1101	e	101	110 0101
&	038	010 0110	[	091	101 1011	m	109	110 1101
'	039	010 0111	\	092	101 1100	n	110	110 1110
(	040	010 1000	]	093	101 1101	x	120	111 1000
)	041	010 1001	^	094	101 1110	y	121	111 1001
?	063	011 1111	_	095	101 1111	z	122	111 1010

(c) A student claims that "All ciphers are breakable given enough time and ciphertext". Explain why the Vernam cipher disproves this statement. [2]

3-18

Section 4

Hardware and software

In this section:

4

Chapter 19 – Hardware and software

Objectives

- Define the terms hardware and software and understand the relationship between them
- Explain what is meant by system software and application software
- Understand the need for, and attributes of, different types of software
- Understand the functions of operating systems, utility programs, libraries and translators

Hardware and software

There is a very simple distinction between computer **hardware** and **software**. Hardware is the term used to describe the electrical or electro-mechanical parts of a computer and its input, output and storage devices.

Software comprises all the programs that are written to make computers function.

In the early days of computing, pioneers like von Neumann (1903-1957) and other (mostly male) engineers, who were figuring out the extremely complex task of how to how to build a computer, thought that the actual coding of programs using binary numbers to represent instructions, and setting the appropriate switches on the machines was a relatively simple task which could be left to young women with suitable secretarial skills and some aptitude for mathematics.

They were soon disabused of this notion. Maurice Wilkes (1913-2010), a computer scientist in the 1940s, recalls:

"As soon as we started programming, we found out to our surprise that it was not as easy to get programs right as we had thought. I can remember the exact instant when I realised that a large part of my life from then on was going to be spent in finding mistakes in my own programs."

Q1: Explain the difference between hardware and software and suggest two examples for each.

Classification of software

Software can be broadly classified into **system software** and **application software**.

System software

System software is the software needed to run the computer's hardware and application programs. This includes the operating system, utility programs, libraries and programming language translators.

Operating system

An operating system is a set of programs that lies between applications software and the computer hardware. It has many different functions, including:

- resource management – managing all the computer hardware including the CPU, memory, disk drives, keyboard, monitor, printer and other peripheral devices
- provision of a user interface (e.g. Windows) to enable users to perform tasks such as running application software, changing settings on the computer, downloading and installing new software.

Operating systems are covered in the next chapter.

4-19

Utility programs

Utility software is system software designed to optimise the performance of the computer or perform tasks such as backing up files, restoring corrupted files from backup, compressing or decompressing data, encrypting data before transmission, providing a firewall, etc.

For example, a **disk defragmenter** is a program that will reorganise a hard disk so that files which have been split up into blocks and stored all over the disk will be recombined in a single series of sequential blocks. This makes reading a file quicker. The software utility *Optimise Drives*, previously called *Disk Defragmenter*, runs automatically on a weekly schedule on the latest versions of Windows. You can also optimise drives on your PC manually.

A **virus checker** utility checks your hard drive and depending on the level of protection offered, incoming emails and internet downloads, for viruses and removes them. Windows 8.1 comes with built-in virus protection called Windows Defender.

Several utility programs such as the disk defragmenter, software uninstaller, backup and restore programs and screensavers are supplied as part of the operating system. Other utility programs such as WinZip for compressing and sharing files have to be purchased from independent suppliers.

Libraries

Library programs are ready-compiled programs which can be run when needed, and which are grouped together in software libraries. In Windows these often have a .dll extension. Most compiled languages have their own libraries of pre-written functions which can be invoked in a defined manner from within the user's program.

> **Q2:** What library programs or routines have you used in any of the programs you have written? How is the library invoked by the program?

Translators

Programming language translators fall into three categories: compilers, interpreters and assemblers. All of them translate program code written by a programmer into machine code which can be run by the computer.

Translators are covered in Chapter 22.

4-19

Application software

Application software consists of programs that perform specific user-oriented tasks. It can be categorised as general purpose, special-purpose or custom-written (bespoke) software.

General-purpose software such as a word-processor, spreadsheet or graphics package, can be used for many different purposes. For example, a graphics package may be used to produce advertisements, manipulate photographs, draw vector or bit-mapped images.

Special-purpose software performs a single specific task or set of tasks. Examples include payroll and accounts packages, hotel booking systems, fingerprint scanning systems, browser software and hundreds of other applications. Software may be bought "**off-the-shelf**", ready to use, or it may be specially written by a team of programmers for a particular organisation. If, say, a hotel wants to buy some visitor booking software, they may be able to find a ready-made package that is quite suitable, or they may want a **bespoke** software package that will satisfy their particular requirements. It will almost certainly be cheaper to buy a ready-made package, even if it contains a lot of features which they will never use, since the cost is shared among all the other people buying the package. It will also have the advantages that it is ready to be installed immediately, and is likely to be well-documented, well-tested and bug-free.

Exercises

1. (a) Software can be classified as either **system** or **application software**. What is meant by

    (i)   system software?   [1]

    (ii)   application software?   [1]

  (b) Give an example of each type of software.   [2]

2. A company sells widgets via an online web store. The process of updating the website and processing sales involves many different types of software.

Below is a list of software:

> **Operating system, Utility software, Special-purpose software, General purpose application software, Bespoke software**

Complete the table below by writing one software category beside each use. You should not use a category more than once.

Software	Category
Firewall software installed on the web server	
Store's own online ordering system designed for their products and systems	
Graphics software to crop product images suitable for uploading to the site	
Online payment verification software	

         [4]

3. Give **two** reasons why a company might choose to purchase a special purpose software package rather than a suite of programs written specifically for their needs.   [2]

4-19

Chapter 20 – Role of an operating system

Objectives

- Understand that the role of the operating system is to hide the complexities of the hardware from the user

- Know that the OS handles resource management, managing hardware to allocate processors, memories and I/O devices among competing processes

What is an operating system?

An operating system is a program or set of programs that manages the operations of the computer for the user. It acts as a bridge between the user and the computer's hardware, since a user cannot communicate with hardware directly.

The operating system is held in permanent storage, for example on a hard disk. A small program called the **loader** is held in ROM. When a computer is switched on, the loader in ROM sends instructions to load the operating system by copying it from storage into RAM.

Functions of an operating system

4-20

Regardless of whether the operating system is embedded within an mp3 player or is the latest version of Windows installed on a desktop computer, all operating systems share the same basic functions.

An operating system disguises the complexities of managing and communicating with its hardware from the user via an **Application Programming Interface (API)**. Through this interface, a user can naively tap away to complete their tasks, (loading, saving or printing for example), oblivious to the actual operations taking place behind the scenes to support their actions.

Apart from providing a user interface, the operating system has to perform the following functions:

- memory management
- processor scheduling
- backing store management
- management of all input and output

We will look at what each of these functions involve.

Q1: A PC is a multitasking machine. What does this mean? Is it the same thing as multiprocessing?

Memory management

A PC allows a user to be working on several tasks at the same time. You may be listening to music via a streaming site such as Spotify, entering a Python program, checking your emails every so often and running Word so that you can document your program design. Meanwhile, a virus checker may be running in the background.

Each program, open file or copied clipboard item, for example, must be allocated a specific area of memory whilst the computer is running. Should a user wish to switch from one application to another in a separate window, each application must be stored in memory simultaneously. The allocation and management of space is controlled by the operating system.

In some cases, the computer's RAM may not be not large enough to store all these programs simultaneously, so the hard disk is used as an extension of memory – called **virtual** memory. MS Word may be open on your desktop but if you are not actually using it at a particular time, the operating system may copy the Word software and data to hard disk to free up RAM for the browser software, the Pascal compiler or whatever you as the user have requested. When you switch back to Word, the operating system will reload it into memory.

Q2: Do you notice that response time slows down on your PC when you have a lot of programs running? What would be the effect of installing more RAM on your computer? Why?

Processor scheduling

With computers able to run multiple applications simultaneously, the operating system is responsible for allocating processor time to each one as they compete for the CPU. While one application is busy using the CPU for processing, the OS can queue up the next process required by another application to make the most efficient use of the processor. A computer with a single-core processor can only process one instruction at a time, but by carrying out small parts of multiple larger tasks in turn, the processor can give the appearance of carrying out several tasks simultaneously. This is what is meant by **multi-tasking**.

The **scheduler** is the operating system module responsible for making sure that processor time is used as efficiently as possible. Of course, this is a much more complex task on a large multi-user system where many users may, for example, be accessing the same database or running different applications on an application server. The objectives of the scheduler are to:

- maximise throughput
- be fair to all users on a multi-user system
- provide acceptable response time to all users
- ensure hardware resources are kept as busy as possible

Q3: There are several different "scheduling algorithms" used by different operating systems. Suggest an algorithm that would achieve the objectives of the scheduler.

Backing store management

When files and applications are loaded, they are transferred from backing storage into memory. The operating system is required to keep a directory of where files are stored so that they can be quickly accessed. Similarly, it needs to know which areas of storage are free so that new files or applications can be saved. The file management system that comes with your desktop operating system enables a user to move files and folders, delete files and protect others from unauthorised access.

Q4: What happens to file access times as the disk becomes very full? Why? What action needs to be taken?

4-20

Peripheral management

Different applications will require different input or output devices throughout their operation. If you send a file to print, the operating system will need to communicate with the printer to check that it is switched on and online, check that it is a printer and not, say, the keyboard and begin communication to send it the correct data to print. The operating system also ensures that peripherals are allocated to processes without causing conflicts.

Interrupt handling

An interrupt is a signal from a peripheral or software program that causes the operating system to stop processing its current list of instructions and think what to do next. Should an error occur such as a software crash or 'out of paper' message from a printer, the OS is responsible for detecting the interrupt signal and displaying an appropriate error message for the user if appropriate. It is because a processor can be interrupted that **multi-tasking** can take place.

Q5: What other events could cause an interrupt?

Exercises

1. Explain the purpose of the operating system. [2]

2. An operating system is designed to hide the complexities of the hardware from the user and to manage the hardware and other resources.

   Give **three** different types of management of either hardware or other resources that are performed by an operating system. [3]

   AQA Comp 3 Qu 1 June 2013

4-20

Chapter 21 – Programming language classification

Objectives

- Be aware of the development of programming languages and their classification into low- and high-level languages

- Describe low-level languages: machine-code and assembly language

- Explain the term 'imperative high-level language' and its relationship to low-level programming

- Understand the advantages and disadvantages of machine-code and assembly language programming compared with high-level programming

Early programmable computers

The first computers were conceived in the 1940s during the Second World War for military purposes – famously, Alan Turing and others at Bletchley Park cracked the Enigma Code used by the Germans with the aid of Colossus, one of the very first programmable computers. By the late 1940s, there was still only a handful of computers in existence but a few large companies were becoming interested in using them for commercial purposes such as payroll; one of the first major computer applications. They discovered that a computer could work out employees' pay about 1000 times faster than a human being.

The Colossus computer

These early computers had very limited memory (with each memory cell made out of a vacuum tube the size of a lightbulb). As well as a collection of memory cells, typically consisting of 16 bits, they had an **accumulator** – a special memory location in which all calculations were carried out – and a **control unit** that decoded instructions. There was only one way of programming a computer; entering the binary digits that the computer could understand. This was called **machine code**.

Machine code

In machine code, a typical instruction holds an operation code (opcode) in the first few bits and an operand in the rest of the memory cell. For example, in an 8-bit instruction set, the first 4 bits might hold the opcode and the other 4 bits will hold the operand (the data to be operated on, or the address where the data is held). In reality, at least 32 bits would usually be used to hold an instruction.

Q1: How many different instructions are possible with 4 bits being used for the op code?

For example, some of the machine code instructions in the instruction set for this imaginary computer might take the form given by the following table:

Instruction	Meaning
0000	Load the value stored in memory location specified by the operand into the accumulator
0001	Store the value in the accumulator in memory location specified by the operand
0010	Add the value specified in the operand to the value in the accumulator
0011	Compare the contents of the accumulator with the contents of the location specified by the operand
0100	Jump to the address held in the operand if the accumulator held the lesser value in the last comparison
0101	Jump to the address held in the operand if the accumulator held the greater value in the last comparison
0110	Jump to the address held in the operand
1000	Stop

Now we can write a machine code program!

Example 1

Lines 1-7 below are part of a machine code program to swap the two numbers held in locations 8 and 9.

```
1  0000 1000
2  0001 1010
3  0000 1001
4  0001 1000
5  0000 1010
6  0001 1001
7  1000 0000
8  0001 1001
9  0001 0111
```

4-21

Q2: Fill in a trace table to show the contents of the accumulator and memory locations 8, 9, 10. The first line has been done. The initial contents of location 10 are unknown.

Accumulator	Location 8	Location 9	Location 10
25	25	23	25
etc.			

It's very easy to see how extremely difficult, tedious and error-prone it was to program in machine code. The same operation can be done in Python, for example, with the statement:

```
x,y = y,x
```

This is a good example of **abstraction** – you really don't want to know all the details of how the computer actually achieves the swap, as it distracts from the task to be performed – and you certainly don't want to have to write out and debug all the machine code instructions. In the Python version, all the details have been abstracted away, leaving you free to concentrate on the algorithm (which could be, for example, a sorting algorithm).

Machine code is called a **low-level programming language**, because the code reflects how the computer actually carries out the instruction – it is dependent on the actual architecture of the computer.

Assembly language

The next stage in the development of programming languages was assembly language, another **low-level language**. This had two major improvements:

1. Each opcode was replaced by a mnemonic which gave a good clue to what the operator was actually doing.
2. The operand was replaced by a decimal (or hexadecimal) number.

The program to swap two numbers now looks like this:

```
1  LDA 8      ;load the contents of location 8 into accumulator
2  STO 10     ;store the contents of the accumulator in location 10
3  LDA 9      ;load the contents of location 9 into accumulator
4  STO 8      ;store the contents of the accumulator in location 8
5  LDA 10     ;load the contents of location 10 into accumulator
6  STO 9      ;store the contents of the accumulator in location 9
7  STOP
8  25         ;data
9  23         ;data
```

This was a major improvement on machine code but still involved coding every step that the computer needed to perform to accomplish each task. The set of mnemonics looked something like this:

Instruction	Meaning
LDA	Load the value stored in memory location specified by the operand into the accumulator
STO	Store the value in the accumulator in memory location specified by the operand
ADD	Add the value specified in the memory location specified by the operand to the value in the accumulator
CMP	Compare the contents of the accumulator with the contents of the location specified by the operand
BLT	Jump to the address held in the operand if the accumulator held the lesser value in the last comparison
BGT	Jump to the address held in the operand if the accumulator held the greater value in the last comparison
JMP	Jump to the address held in the operand
STOP	Stop

Q3: Write an assembly language program to add the two numbers in locations 8 and 9 and store the result in location 10.

4-21

High-level programming languages

In the 1960s, John Backus and his team at IBM made a hugely significant breakthrough in the development of programming. Backus saw that what was needed was a programming language that enabled programmers to write programs in the same way that they wrote algorithms or mathematical formulae. The first high-level language was born, and they called it **FORTRAN**, short for FORmula TRANslation. Other languages such as ALGOL, BASIC and COBOL soon followed.

In a high-level language, programmers could write statements such as

```
X = (B - C) * D
```

These languages are all examples of **imperative high-level languages**, so-called because each instruction is basically a command to perform some step in the program, which consists of the step-by-step instructions needed to complete the task. They are **high-level** because they enable programmers to think and code in terms of algorithms, without worrying about how each tiny step will be executed in machine code and where each item of data will be stored. Each instruction in a high level language is translated into several low-level language instructions.

The advantages of high-level languages compared to a low-level language include the following:

- They are relatively easy to learn
- It is much easier and faster to write a program in a high-level language
- Programs written in high-level languages are much easier to understand, debug and maintain
- Programs written in a high-level language are not dependent on the architecture of a particular machine – they are machine independent
- There are many built-in library functions available in most high-level languages
- Different high-level languages are often written specifically for a particular class of problem; for example SQL is tailor-made for querying and manipulating databases

The assembly language program on the previous page to swap two numbers would be written using high-level language as:

```
a ← 25
b ← 23
c ← b
a ← b
b ← c
```

Assembly language is still used when the program needs to execute as fast as possible, occupy as little space as possible or manipulate individual bits and bytes. Examples include embedded systems, real-time systems, sensors, mobile phones, device drivers and interrupt handlers.

Exercises

1. (a) A machine code instruction can be split into an opcode part and an operand part.

    (i) What does an opcode represent? [1]

    (ii) What does an operand represent? [1]

  (b) State **two** advantages of writing a program in assembly language over writing a program in machine code. [2]

AQA Comp 2 Qu 2 June 2012

4-21

Chapter 22 – Programming language translators

Objectives

- Understand the role of an assembler, compiler and interpreter

- Explain the difference between compilation and interpretation, and describe situations when both would be appropriate

- Explain why an intermediate language such as bytecode is produced as the final output by some compilers and how it is subsequently used

- Understand the difference between source and object (executable) code

Assembler

In the last chapter we looked at machine code and assembly language. Both of these are **low-level languages,** with each instruction in assembly language almost always being equivalent to one machine code instruction. The machine code instructions that a particular computer can execute (the **instruction set**) are completely dependent on its hardware, and therefore each different type of processor will have a different instruction set and a different assembly language.

Before an assembly language program can be executed, it must be translated into the equivalent machine code. This is done by a program called an **assembler**. The assembler program takes each assembly language instruction and converts it to the 0s and 1s of the corresponding machine code instruction. The input to the assembler is called the **source code** and the output (machine code) the **object code**.

Compiler

A compiler is a program that translates a high-level language such as Visual Basic, C#, Python etc. into machine code. The code written by the programmer, the **source code**, is input as data to the compiler, which scans through it several times, each time performing different checks and building up tables of information needed to produce the final object code. Different hardware platforms will require different compilers, since the resulting object code will be hardware-specific. For example, Windows and the Intel microprocessors comprise one platform, Apple and ARM processors another, so separate compilers are required for each.

The object code can then be saved and run whenever needed without the presence of the compiler.

INPUT	PROCESS	OUPUT
Source code e.g. Python program	Compile	Object code (executable machine code)

Interpreter

An interpreter is a different type of programming language translator. The interpreter software itself contains subroutines to carry out each high-level instruction. Once the programmer has written and saved a program, and instructs the computer to run it, the interpreter looks at each line of the source program, analyses it and, if it contains no syntax errors, calls the appropriate subroutine within its own program code to execute the command.

For example, the following Python program contains an error at line 5.

```
1  a = 1
2  b = 2
3  c = a + b
4  print("a + b = ", c)
5  d = a - n
6  print("a - b = ", d)
7  print("goodbye")
```

When the program runs, it produces the following output:

```
a + b = 3
Traceback (most recent call last):
   File "C:/Users/A Level sample programs/prog1.py", line 5, in <module>
      d = a - n
NameError: name 'n' is not defined
```

The program produces output at line 4, gets as far as line 5 and then crashes.

However, it is not always quite that simple. If we modify the program to introduce a syntax error at line 6, (missing closing bracket) the interpreter does not attempt to run any of the program until this is fixed.

```
1  a = 1
2  b = 2
3  c = a + b
4  print("a + b = ", c)
5  e = a - b
6  print("a - b = ", d
7  print("goodbye")
```

When the program runs, it does not execute any of the code but produces the following output:

From this we can deduce that the translator has scanned through the whole program checking for certain types of error before executing any of it.

Bytecode

Interpreting each line of code just before executing it has become much less common. Most interpreted languages such as Python and Java use an intermediate representation which combines compiling and interpreting. The resulting **bytecode** is then executed by a **bytecode interpreter**.

The bytecode may be compiled once and for all (as in Java) or each time a change in the source code is detected before execution (as in Python).

A big advantage of bytecode is that you can achieve **platform independence**; any computer that can run Java programs has a **Java Virtual Machine (JVM)**, a piece of software which masks inherent differences between different computer architectures and operating systems. The JVM understands bytecode and converts it into the machine code for that particular computer.

A second advantage of using, for example, Java bytecode is that it acts as an extra security layer between your computer and the program. You can download an untrusted program and you then execute the Java bytecode interpreter rather than the program itself, which guards against any malicious programs.

It is also possible to compile from Python into Java bytecode (using the Jython compiler) and then use the Java interpreter to interpret and execute it.

Advantages and uses of compilers and interpreters

A compiler has many advantages over an interpreter:

- the object code can be saved on disk and run whenever required without the need to recompile. However, if an error is discovered in the program, the whole program has to be recompiled

- the object code executes faster than interpreted code

- the object code produced by a compiler can be distributed or executed without having to have the compiler present

- the object code is more secure, as it cannot be read without a great deal of 'reverse engineering'

A compiler would therefore be appropriate when a program is to be run regularly or frequently, with only occasional change. It is also appropriate when the object code produced by the compiler is going to be distributed or sold to users outside the company that produced the software, since the source code is not present and therefore cannot be copied or amended.

> **Q1:** Why would a company or an individual programmer not want to distribute the source code when they sell a software package?

An interpreter has some advantages over a compiler:

- it is useful for program development as there is no need for lengthy recompilation each time an error is discovered

- it is easier to partially test and debug programs

However, the program may run slower than a compiled program, because each statement has to be translated to machine code each time it is encountered. So if a loop of 10 statements is performed 20 times, all 10 statements are interpreted 20 times.

An interpreter may, for example, be used during program development and when the program is complete and correct, it can be compiled for distribution or regular use within the company. An interpreter may also be used in a student environment when students are learning code, as they can test parts of a program before coding it all.

4-22

Exercises

1. A programmer is asked to write a program and can choose between using a low-level language or a high-level procedural language.

   Outline the major difference between these two types of languages, naming an example of each.

   For each language explain:

   - advantages and disadvantages of each one compared to the other

   - what translation software would be used, if applicable

   - a situation when each one would be the most appropriate choice   [10]

2. Explain why an intermediate language such as bytecode is produced as the final output by some compilers and how it is subsequently used.   [5]

3. (a) The high-level language statement

   A := B + 5

   is to be written in assembly language.

   Complete the following assembly language statements, which are to be the equivalent of the above high level language statement. The `Load` and `Store` instructions imply the use of the accumulator register.

   ```
   Load  .............................
   .................................#5
   Store  ..........................
   ```
                  [3]

   (b) (i) What type of translator is required to translate assembly language statements into machine code?   [1]

   (ii) What type of translator is required to translate a high-level language statement into machine code?   [1]

   AQA Comp2 Qu 3 January 2009

4-22

Chapter 23 – Logic gates

Objectives

- Construct truth tables for a variety of logic gates
- Be familiar with drawing and interpreting logic gate circuit diagrams involving multiple gates
- Complete a truth table for a given logic gate circuit
- Write a Boolean expression for a given logic gate circuit
- Draw an equivalent logic gate circuit for a given Boolean expression

Binary logic

At the most elementary level, an electronic device can only recognise the presence or absence of current or voltage. Either electricity is present or it isn't. This is a switch – on or off, true or false, 1 or 0. With a computer's semiconductor, the voltage at the input and output terminals is measured and is either high or low; 1 or 0. Computers comprise billions of these switches and manipulating these sequences of Ons and Offs can change individual bits.

Electronic logic gates can take one or more inputs and produce a single output. This output can become the input to another gate and a complicated cascaded sequence of logic gates can be implemented to form a circuit in, for example, the CPU.

Simple logic gates and truth tables

There are a number of different logic gates that are each designed to perform a different operation in terms of output. These are: NOT, AND, OR, XOR, NAND and NOR gates. Each of these gates can be represented by a truth table showing the output given for each possible input or combination of inputs. The first three gates are shown below. Inputs are usually given algebraic letters such as A, B and C and output is usually represented by P or Q.

NOT gate

The NOT gate is represented by the symbol below and inverts the input. The small circle denotes an inverted input.

Using 1s and 0s as inputs to a gate, its operation can summarised in the form of a **truth table**.

Q = NOT A

Input A	Output Q
0	1
1	0

The Boolean algebraic expression is written: $Q = \overline{A}$ where the overbar $\overline{}$ represents NOT.

AND gate

Q = A AND B

Input A	Input B	Output Q
0	0	0
0	1	0
1	0	0
1	1	1

The Boolean expression for AND is written: $Q = A \cdot B$ where $\cdot$ represents AND.

The truth table reflects the fundamental property of the AND gate: the output of A AND B is 1 only if input A and input B are both 1.

OR gate

Q = A OR B

Input A	Input B	Output Q
0	0	0
0	1	1
1	0	1
1	1	1

The Boolean expression for OR is written: $Q = A + B$ where $+$ represents OR.

Creating logic gate circuits

Multiple logic gates can be connected to produce an output based on multiple inputs.

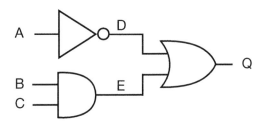

This circuit can be represented by $Q = (NOT\ A)\ OR\ (B\ AND\ C)$ or $Q = \overline{A} + (B \cdot C)$ and shown using the truth table below:

Input A	Input B	Input C	D = NOT A	E = B AND C	Output Q = (NOT A) OR (B AND C)
0	0	0	1	0	1
0	0	1	1	0	1
0	1	0	1	0	1
0	1	1	1	1	1
1	0	0	0	0	0
1	0	1	0	0	0
1	1	0	0	0	0
1	1	1	0	1	1

Q1: Draw a truth table for the following circuit:

4-23

The XOR, NAND and NOR gates

XOR gate

The XOR (*pronounced ex-or*) gate stands for exclusive OR, meaning that the output will be true if one or other input is true, but not both. Compare this to the OR gate, which outputs true if either or both inputs are true.

Q = A XOR B

Input A	Input B	Output Q
0	0	0
0	1	1
1	0	1
1	1	0

The Boolean algebraic expression is written: $Q = A \oplus B$ where the $\oplus$ represents XOR, and is the equivalent of $Q = (A \cdot \overline{B}) + (\overline{A} \cdot B)$. This gate is similar to the OR gate but excludes the condition where A and B are both true. For this reason the OR gate is sometimes referred to as an inclusive OR.

Q2: Show, by drawing a truth table for $P = (A \cdot \overline{B}) + (\overline{A} \cdot B)$, that $P = Q$, where $Q = A \oplus B$.

The XOR gate performs the function of an addition of the two inputs and combined with an AND gate, will output the carry bit value as well.

NAND gate

The NAND gate is an amalgamation of the AND and NOT gates, which inverts the output of the AND gate. Having a single type of NAND gate that can perform two separate functions can help to reduce development costs if a NAND gate is cheaper than separate AND and NOT gates.

Q = NOT (A AND B)

Input A	Input B	Output Q
0	0	1
0	1	1
1	0	1
1	1	0

The Boolean algebraic expression is written: $Q = \overline{A \cdot B}$.

NOR gate

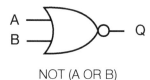

NOT (A OR B)

Input A	Input B	Output Q
0	0	1
0	1	0
1	0	0
1	1	0

The Boolean algebraic expression is written: $Q = \overline{A + B}$. This gate only produces an output of true when both inputs are false.

Q3: Compare the truth table outputs of the AND and NAND gates, and the OR with the NOR. How do these differ?

Q4: Draw a logic circuit for the expression Q = NOT ((A XOR B) AND C), i.e. $Q = \overline{(A \oplus B) \cdot C}$

Exercises

1. (a) Complete the following truth tables for the NAND, NOR and XOR logic gates.

NAND gate

Input A	Input B	Output Q
0	0	
0	1	
1	0	
1	1	

[1]

NOR gate

Input A	Input B	Output Q
0	0	
0	1	
1	0	
1	1	

[1]

XOR gate

Input A	Input B	Output Q
0	0	
0	1	
1	0	
1	1	

[1]

4-23

(b) Draw logic circuits for the following Boolean expressions:

  (i) $Q = A \oplus B + \overline{B}$ [3]

  (ii) $Q = \overline{A} \cdot B + C$ [3]

  (iii) $Q = \overline{A + B} + (A \cdot C)$ [3]

2. The figure below shows a logic circuit.

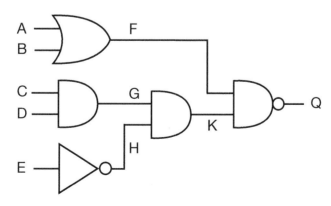

(a) Write the equivalent Boolean expression.   [3]

(b) What are the values of F, G, H, K and Q if A, B, C and D and E are all equal 1?   [5]

Chapter 24 – Boolean algebra

Objectives

- Be familiar with the use of Boolean identities and De Morgan's laws to manipulate and simplify Boolean expressions

- Write a Boolean expression for a given logic gate circuit, and vice versa

De Morgan's laws

Augustus de Morgan (1806-1871) was a Cambridge Mathematics professor who formulated two theorems or laws relating to logic. These laws can be used to manipulate and simplify Boolean expressions. Although his theoretical work had little practical application in his lifetime, it became of major significance in the next century in the field of digital electronics, in which TRUE and FALSE can be replaced by ON and OFF or the binary numbers 0 and 1.

Using de Morgan's laws, any Boolean function can be converted to one which uses only NAND functions or only NOR functions, and these can be further converted to an expression using all NAND functions or all NOR functions.

Thus, any integrated circuit can be built from just one type of logic gate. This is an advantage in manufacturing where costs can be kept down by using only one type of gate.

De Morgan's first law

$$\overline{A + B} = \overline{A} \cdot \overline{B}$$

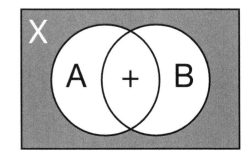

The truth of this is clear from the Venn diagram on the right. Suppose we have a variable X defined by

$$X = \overline{A + B}$$

Looking at the Venn diagram, A + B is represented by the white area. Since X is not in A + B, it consists of all the shaded area. This can be defined as everything not in A and not in B, i.e.

$$X = \overline{A} \cdot \overline{B}$$

Q1: Complete the following truth table to show that $\overline{A + B} = \overline{A} \cdot \overline{B}$

A	B	$\overline{A}$	$\overline{B}$	A + B	$\overline{A + B}$	$\overline{A} \cdot \overline{B}$
0	0					
0	1					
1	0					
1	1					

De Morgan's second law

$$\overline{A \cdot B} = \overline{A} + \overline{B}$$

Again, looking at the Venn diagram on the right, if

$$X = \overline{A \cdot B}$$

X cannot be in the white area, so must be in the red, orange, or shaded areas. That is, X is either not in A, or not in B, or not in either. This is the definition of

$$X = \overline{A} + \overline{B}$$

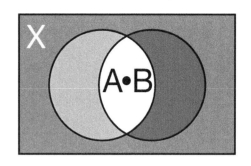

Q2: Complete the following truth table to show that $\overline{A \cdot B} = \overline{A} + \overline{B}$

A	B	$\overline{A}$	$\overline{B}$	$A \cdot B$	$\overline{A \cdot B}$	$\overline{A} + \overline{B}$
0						
0						
1						
1						

To implement each of de Morgan's laws to find $\overline{A + B}$, or $\overline{A \cdot B}$, follow the three steps:

1. Complement both terms in the expression, e.g. A, B
2. Change AND to OR and OR to AND
3. Invert the result

Drawing circuits using NAND and NOR gates

We saw in the last chapter that a NAND gate is equivalent a combination of an AND gate and a NOT gate.

$Q = NOT\ (A\ AND\ B)$, which is the same as $Q = \overline{A \cdot B}$

Likewise, a NOR gate is a combination of an OR gate and a NOT gate.

$Q = NOT\ (A\ OR\ B)$, which is the same as $Q = \overline{A + B}$

Q3: Using only NAND and NOR gates and with the aid of de Morgan's laws, draw circuits for

(i)　　$Q = \overline{A} + \overline{B}$

(ii)　　$Q = \overline{A} \cdot \overline{B}$

Rules of Boolean algebra

In addition to de Morgan's laws, there are several identities or "rules" which will help you to simplify Boolean expressions. The most useful are listed below.

General rules

1. $X \cdot 0 = 0$
2. $X \cdot 1 = X$
3. $X \cdot X = X$
4. $X \cdot \overline{X} = 0$
5. $X + 0 = X$
6. $X + 1 = 1$
7. $X + X = X$
8. $X + \overline{X} = 1$
9. $\overline{\overline{X}} = X$

Commutative rules

10. $X \cdot Y = Y \cdot X$
11. $X + Y = Y + X$

Associative rules

12. $X \cdot (Y \cdot Z) = (X \cdot Y) \cdot Z$
13. $X + (Y + Z) = (X + Y) + Z$

Distributive rules

14. $X \cdot (Y + Z) = X \cdot Y + X \cdot Z$
15. $(X + Y) \cdot (W + Z) = X \cdot W + X \cdot Z + Y \cdot W + Y \cdot Z$

Absorption rules

16. $X + (X \cdot Y) = X$
17. $X \cdot (X + Y) = X$

Note: $X \cdot Y$ can be written as XY and vice versa.

Example 1

Use de Morgan's laws and the rules of Boolean algebra to simplify the following Boolean expression:

$$Q = \overline{\overline{(X \cdot \overline{Y})} \cdot \overline{(\overline{Y} + Z)}}$$

Answer: $Q = (X \cdot \overline{Y}) + (\overline{\overline{Y} + Z})$ (using de Morgan's second law)

                $= (X \cdot \overline{Y}) + (Y \cdot \overline{Z})$ (using de Morgan's first law)

This is an acceptably simplified answer. It could also be expressed as:

$$Q = X \cdot \overline{Y} + Y \cdot \overline{Z}$$

Example 2

Use de Morgan's laws to simplify $A \cdot B + \overline{A} + \overline{B}$

Answer: The expression is equivalent to:

         $A \cdot B + \overline{A \cdot B}$ (using de Morgan's first law)

         $= 1$ (using rule 8 above)

4-24

Q4: Use de Morgan's laws to simplify $\overline{A} + \overline{B} + \overline{(A + B)}$

Example 3

Use Boolean algebra to show that $(A + B) \cdot (A + C) = A + B \cdot C$

Answer:

$$(A + B) \cdot (A + C) = A \cdot A + B \cdot A + B \cdot C + A \cdot C \qquad \text{(distributive rule)}$$

$$= A + B \cdot A + B \cdot C + A \cdot C \qquad \text{(since A.A = A for rule number 3)}$$

$$= A + A \cdot B + A \cdot C + B \cdot C \qquad \text{(commutative rule)}$$

$$= A \cdot (1 + B + C) + B \cdot C \qquad \text{(distributive rule)}$$

$$= A + B \cdot C \qquad \text{(rules 2 and 6)}$$

The final line makes use of the fact that anything OR'd with 1 is 1.

Q5: Draw a truth table to show that $(A + B) \cdot (A + C) = A + B \cdot C$

Q6: Use Boolean algebra and de Morgan's laws to show that: $A \cdot (A + B) = A$

Example 4

A single output Q is produced from three inputs X, Y and Z. Q is 1 only if X and Y are 1, or Z is 1 and Y is 0.

Write the Boolean expression to represent this circuit.

Answer: There are three separate logic gates involved here: X AND Y, Z AND (NOT Y). The output from these three gates are input to an OR gate.

$$Q = (X \cdot Y) + (Z \cdot \overline{Y})$$

4-24

Represent this equation diagrammatically using a combination of AND, OR and NOT gates.

Answer:

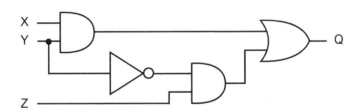

Example 5

Write the Boolean expression corresponding to the following logic circuit.

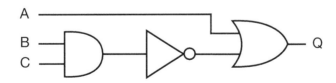

Answer: $A + \overline{(B \cdot C)}$

Q7: Replace two of the gates in the above circuit with a single gate.

Q8: The NAND gate is a universal gate. Can you work out how to make combinations of NAND gates act like NOT, AND and OR gates? (Look up "universal NAND gate" on Google for help!)

Exercises

1. Figure 1 below shows a logic circuit.

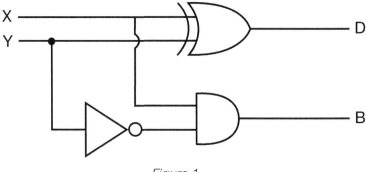

Figure 1

(a) Write a Boolean expression for **D**. [1]

(b) Write a Boolean expression for **B**. [1]

(c) Figure 2 below shows a different logic circuit.

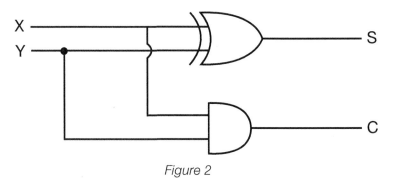

Figure 2

(i) Complete the truth table for the logic circuit shown in Figure 2.

Inputs		Outputs	
X	**Y**	**C**	**S**
0	0		
0	1		
1	0		
1	1		

[2]

(ii) What arithmetic function does the logic circuit in **Figure 2** perform? [1]

(d) Without using a truth table, simplify the Boolean expression below.

$(X + Y) \cdot (X + \overline{Y})$

Show the stages of your working. [3]

AQA Comp 2 Qu 2 January 2012

4-24

Exercises continued

2. (a) Complete the truth tables for the following logic gates. [2]

AND gate				XOR gate		
Input X	**Input Y**	**Output Q**		**Input X**	**Input Y**	**Output Q**
0	0			0	0	
0	1			0	1	
1	0			1	0	
1	1			1	1	

(b) A line-following robot has three sensors. It moves along a black line on a white background whilst the following conditions are met:

- the ultrasonic sensor U does not detect any obstacle
- either, but not both, of the infrared sensors L and R are on the black line.

Sensor U returns 1 if it detects an obstacle and 0 if the path is clear.

Sensors L and R each return 1 if they detect black and 0 if they detect white.

A logic circuit will process the input from the sensors and produce an output M.

M should be 1 if the robot is to move and 0 if the robot should stop.

(i) Represent the output M as a Boolean expression. [3]

(ii) The following symbols are used to represent logic gates:

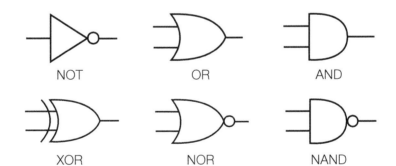

Using a combination of any of the above logic gates draw a logic circuit for this system in the box below. You will not need to use all of the different types of logic gates.

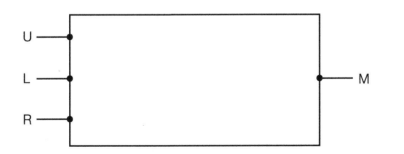

[3]

(c) Apply de Morgan's laws to the following expression and simplify the result.

$$Q = \overline{\overline{A} + \overline{(B \cdot A)}}$$

Show the stages of your working. [3]

AQA Comp 2 Qu 8 June 2012

3. (a) State the names of the logic gates represented by each of the three truth tables below.

Input A	Input B	Output
0	0	0
0	1	0
1	0	0
1	1	1

Logic gate name:

Input A	Input B	Output
0	0	1
0	1	0
1	0	0
1	1	0

Logic gate name:

Input A	Input B	Output
0	0	0
0	1	1
1	0	1
1	1	0

Logic gate name: [3]

(b) Simplify the following Boolean expressions.

   (i) $B \cdot (A + \overline{A})$ [1]

   (ii) $A \cdot B + B$ [1]

   (iii) $\overline{B} \cdot (\overline{\overline{A} + \overline{B}})$ [2]

(c) Draw a logic circuit for the following Boolean expression:

$$Q = A \oplus B \cdot B$$

You will need to make use of the symbols below when drawing your logic circuit.

[2]

AQA Comp 2 Qu 6 June 2013

4-24

Section 5

Computer organisation and architecture

In this section:

5

Chapter 25 – Internal computer hardware

Objectives

- List the basic internal components of a computer system
- Understand the role of the processor, main memory, buses and I/O controllers and how they relate to each other
- Understand the need for, and the means of communication between components
- Explain the difference between von Neumann and Harvard architectures and describe where each is typically used
- Understand the concept of addressable memory
- Describe the stored program concept

Introduction

A computer system has both **internal components** – those within the Central Processing Unit (CPU) – and **external components** such as input/output and storage devices. This chapter describes the internal components. These include:

- processor
- main memory
- address bus, control bus, data bus
- I/O controllers

A simplified block diagram of these components is shown below.

The internal components of a computer

5-25

The Processor

The processor responds to and processes the instructions that drive the computer. It contains the **control unit**, the **arithmetic/logic unit (ALU)** and **registers**.

The control unit coordinates and controls all the operations carried out by the computer. It operates by repeating three operations:

Fetch – causes the next instruction to be fetched from main memory

Decode – decodes the instruction

Execute – causes the instruction to be executed

The ALU can perform different sorts of operations on data. **Arithmetic** operations include addition, subtraction, multiplication and division. **Logical** operations consist of comparing one data item with another to determine whether the first data item is smaller than, equal to or greater than the second data item. Bitwise logical operations (AND, OR etc.) and shift operations can manipulate individual bits.

Registers are special memory cells that operate at very high speed. All arithmetic and logical operations take place within registers.

Buses

A bus is a set of parallel wires connecting two or more components of a computer.

The processor is connected to main memory by three separate **buses**. When the CPU wishes to access a particular main memory location, it sends this address to memory on the **address bus**. The data in that location is then returned to the CPU on the **data bus**. Control signals are sent along the **control bus**.

In the figure below, you can see that data, address and control buses connect the processor, memory and I/O controllers. These three buses are known collectively as the **system bus**. Each bus is a shared transmission medium, so that only one device can transmit along a bus at any one time.

Data and control signals travel in both directions between the processor, memory and I/O controllers. Addresses, on the other hand, travel only one way along the address bus: the processor sends the address of an instruction, or of data to be stored or retrieved, to memory or to an I/O controller.

5-25

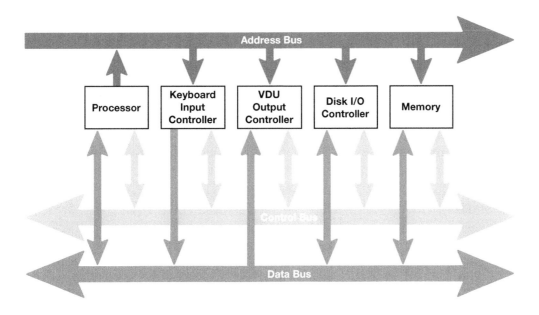

Direction of transmission along the buses

> **Q1:** Which of the data buses in the figure above are uni-directional? Explain why this is the case. What direction does data flow to/from (i) a mouse controller? (ii) a touchscreen controller?

Control bus

The control bus is a bi-directional bus, meaning that signals can be carried in both directions. The data and address buses are shared by all components of the system. Control lines must therefore be provided to ensure that access to and use of the data and address buses by the different components of the system does not lead to conflict.

The purpose of the control bus is to transmit command, timing and specific status information between system components.

Control lines include:

- *Memory Write:* causes data on the data bus to be written into the addressed location
- *Memory Read:* causes data from the addressed location to be placed on the data bus
- *Interrupt request:* indicates that a device is requesting access to the CPU
- *Bus Request:* indicates that a device is requesting the use of the data bus
- *Bus Grant:* indicates that the CPU has granted access to the data bus
- *Clock:* used to synchronise operations
- *Reset:* initialises all components

Data bus

The data bus, typically consisting of 8, 16, 32 or 64 separate lines provides a bi-directional path for moving data and instructions between system components. **The width of the data bus is a key factor in determining overall system performance.** For example, if the data bus is 8 bits wide, and each instruction is 16 bits long, then the processor must access the main memory twice just to fetch the instruction.

Address bus

Memory is divided up internally into units called words. A **word** is a fixed size group of digits, typically 8, 16, 32 or 64 bits, which is handled as a unit by the processor, and different types of processor have different word sizes.

Each word in memory has its own specific address.

When the processor wishes to read a word of data from memory, it first puts the address of the desired word on the address bus. **The width of the address bus determines the maximum possible memory capacity of the system.** For example, if the address bus consisted of only 8 lines, then the maximum address it could transmit would be (in binary) 11111111 or 255, giving a maximum memory capacity of 256 (including address 0). A system with a 32-bit address bus can address 2^{32} (4,294,967,296) memory locations giving an addressable memory space of 4GiB.

The address bus is also used to address I/O ports during input/output operations.

> **Q2:** A 64-bit computer with a 64-bit address bus could theoretically address 16.8 million tebibytes. Is this a practical proposition? Justify your answer.

5-25

No of address lines, m	Maximum no of addressable cells	Maximum no of addressable cells expressed as a power of two, 2^m
1	2	2^1
2	4	2^2
3	8	2^3
4	16	2^4
8	256	2^8
16	65536	2^{16}
20	1048576	2^{20}
24	16777216	2^{24}
.	.	.
.	.	.
.	.	.
32	4,294,967,296	2^{32}

Relationship between number of address lines m and maximum number of addressable memory cells

I/O Controllers

An I/O controller is a device which interfaces between an input or output device and the processor. Each device has a separate controller which connects to the control bus. I/O controllers receive input and output requests from the processor, and then send device-specific control signals to the device they control. They also manage the data flow to and from the device.

The controller is an electronic circuit board consisting of three parts:

* an interface that allows connection of the controller to the system or I/O bus

* a set of data, command and status registers

* an interface that enables connection of the controller to the cable connecting the device to the computer

An **interface** is a standardised form of connection defining such things as signals, number of connecting pins/sockets and voltage levels that appear at the interface. An example is a Universal Serial Bus (USB) connection, which can be used with many different peripherals.

Memory and the stored program concept

Computers as we know them were first built in the 1940s, and two of the early pioneers were Alan Turing and John von Neumann. The **von Neumann architecture** specifies the basic components of the computer and processor in which a shared memory and bus is used for both data and instructions.

The **stored progam concept** can be defined as follows: *machine code instructions are fetched and executed serially by a processor that performs arithmetic and logical operations.*

* A program must be resident in main memory to be executed
* The machine code instructions are fetched from memory one at a time, decoded and executed in the processor

Virtually all computers today are built on this principle, and so the general structure as shown in the figure below is sometimes referred to as the **von Neumann machine**.

5-25

Memory

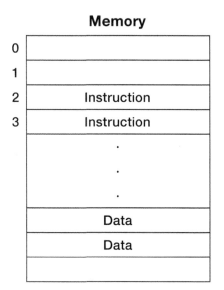

0	
1	
2	Instruction
3	Instruction
	.
	.
	.
	Data
	Data

The von Neumann machine

Harvard architecture

The Harvard architecture is a computer architecture with physically separate memories for instructions and data. Harvard architecture is used extensively with embedded **Digital Signal Processing** (DSP) systems.

The two different memories can have different characteristics; for example, in **embedded systems** instructions may be held in read-only memory while data memory requires read-write memory. In some systems, there is much more instruction memory than data memory so the instruction addresses and address bus are wider than the data addresses and data bus. **Embedded systems** include special-purpose computers built in to devices often operating in real time, such as those used in navigation systems, traffic lights, aircraft flight control systems and simulators.

Harvard architecture can be faster than von Neumann architecture because data and instructions can be fetched in parallel instead of competing for the same bus.

Harvard architecture

Exercises

1.   The data bus, control bus and address bus are three important parts of a modern computer.

(a) In this context, explain what is meant by the term *bus*.   [2]

(b) Fill in the gaps in the paragraph below.

The data bus can be used to transfer data and .... between the main memory and the processor. The control bus carries control signals. An example of a control signal is ....

(c) **Figure 1** shows some of the internal components of a computer system.

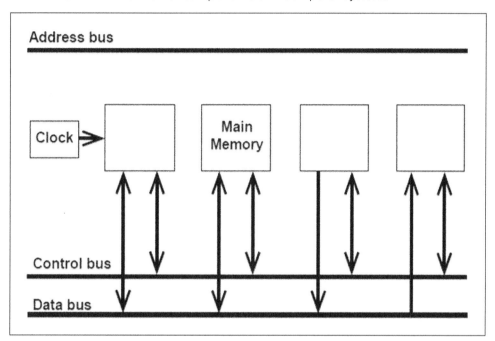

Figure 1

On **Figure 1** label the following components.

Processor, Keyboard controller, Graphics controller

Draw **all** the connections between the address bus and the components. Make sure that you **clearly** show the direction of each connection.   [5]

AQA Comp2 Qu 2 January 2013

2. The program below is written in a low-level language.

```
AB1C  ;Load value 1C into accumulator
BD3E  ;Store contents of accumulator at address 3E
E405  ;Add 5 to the accumulator
BDFF  ;Store contents of accumulator at address FF
AC42  ;Load accumulator with contents of address 42
BD3F  ;Store contents of accumulator at address 3F
```

(a) What is the name of this language?   [1]

(b) The machine for which this program is written has limited addressing capability.

What are the highest and lowest memory addresses that can be addressed by this machine?   [2]

(c) What is the width of the address bus in this machine?   [1]

5-25

Chapter 26 – The processor

Objectives

- Explain the role and operation of the processor and its major components
- Describe the Fetch-Execute cycle
- Describe the factors affecting processor performance

Components of the processor

The processor components were briefly described in the last chapter – here their operation is described in more detail.

Arithmetic Logic Unit (ALU)

The ALU performs arithmetic and logical operations on the data. It can perform instructions such as ADD, SUBTRACT, MULTIPLY, DIVIDE on fixed or floating point numbers. It can also perform shift operations, shifting bits to the left or right within a register. It can carry out Boolean logic operations, comparing two values and using operators such as AND, OR, NOT, XOR.

Control Unit

The Control Unit controls and coordinates the activities of the CPU, directing the flow of data between the CPU and other devices. It accepts the next instruction, breaks down its processing into several sequential steps such as fetching addresses and data from memory, manages its execution and stores the resulting data back in memory or registers.

The system clock

The system clock generates a series of signals, switching between 0 and 1 billions of times per second and synchronising CPU operations. A 3GHz processor's clock ticks three billion times per second. Each CPU operation starts as the clock changes from 0 to 1 (or in some systems from 1 to 0), and the CPU cannot perform operations faster than the clock cycle (the time the clock takes to go from 0 to 1 and back to 0). Some CPU operations take multiple clock cycles.

General-purpose registers

There are typically up to 16 general purpose registers in the CPU. All arithmetic, logical or shift operations take place in registers, which are very fast memory numbered, for example, R0 to R15.

For example, instructions to add the value held in location 164 to the number held in location 150 and store the result in location 170 might take the form:

Load contents of 150 into R1

Add contents of 164 to R1

Store contents of R1 in 170

An **accumulator** is another word for a general purpose register, generally only used when there is just a single register in which to store the result of each calculation or logical expression. Although most modern computers have many registers, some special-purpose processors still use a single accumulator, in order to simplify the design.

Dedicated registers

These include:

- the **program counter (PC)**, which holds the address of the next instruction to be executed. This may be the next instruction in a sequence of instructions, or, if the current instruction is a branch or jump instruction, the address to jump to, (copied from the current instruction register to the PC).

- the **current instruction register (CIR)**, which holds the current instruction being executed.

- the **memory address register (MAR)**, which holds the **address** of the memory location from which data (or an instruction) is to be fetched or to which data is to be written.

- the **memory buffer register (MBR)**, which is used to temporarily store the **data** read from or written to memory. It is also sometimes known as the **memory data register**.

- the **status register (SR)**, which contains bits that are set or cleared depending on the result of an instruction. For example, one bit will be set if an overflow has occurred, other bits will indicate whether the result of the last instruction was negative, zero or caused a carry.

The following block diagram shows these components.

The Fetch-Execute cycle

The sequence of operations involved in executing an instruction can be divided into three phases – **fetching**, **decoding** and **executing** it. This cycle is repeated over and over as each instruction of the program is executed.

How the registers are used in the Fetch-Execute cycle

(Fetch phase)

1. The address of the next instruction is copied from the program counter (PC) to the memory address register (MAR). The address is sent via the address bus to main memory.

2. The instruction held at that address is returned along the data bus to the memory buffer register (MBR). Simultaneously, the content of the PC is incremented so that it holds the address of the next instruction.

3. The contents of the MBR are copied to the current instruction register (CIR).

(Decode phase)

4. The instruction held in the CIR is decoded. The instruction is split into opcode and operand and the opcode is used to determine the type of instruction and what hardware to use to execute it. Additional data is fetched if necessary, and passed to the registers.

(Execute phase)

5. The instruction is executed, using the ALU if necessary, and results are stored in the accumulator, general purpose register or memory.

5-26

Q1: Draw a flowchart showing the steps in the fetch-execute cycle.

Q2: Assume that each machine code instruction is held in one word of memory. When a sequence of instructions is performed, at Step 2 of the Fetch phase above, the PC is incremented by 1 to point to the instruction in the next word of memory. When would the PC not simply be incremented by 1 in order to hold the address of the next instruction?

Factors affecting processor performance

The main factors affecting processor performance are:

- The number of **cores** linked together on a single chip
- The amount and type of cache memory
- Clock speed
- Word length
- Address bus width
- Data bus width

Number of cores

In a traditional computer (von Neumann machine) instructions are fetched and executed one at a time in a serial manner. However, many computers nowadays have multiple cores, having for example, a **dual-core** or **quad-core** processor.

Each core is theoretically able to process a different instruction at the same time with its own fetch-execute cycle, making it two or even four times faster with a quad-core chip. However, although a dual-core processor has twice the power, it does not always perform twice as fast, because the software may not be able to take full advantage of both processors.

Amount and type of cache memory

Cache is a very small amount of expensive, very fast memory inside or very near to the CPU. When an instruction is fetched from main memory it is copied into the cache so if it is needed again soon after, it can be fetched from cache, which is much quicker than going back to main memory. As cache fills up, unused instructions or data still being held are replaced with more recent ones.

There are different "levels" of cache:

- Level 1 cache is extremely fast but small (between 2-64KB)
- Level 2 cache is fairly fast and medium-sized (256KB-2MB)
- Some CPU's also have Level 3 cache

Clock speed

All processor activities begin on a clock pulse, although some activities may take more than one clock cycle to complete. One clock cycle per second = 1 Hertz (Hz), and clock speed is measured in Gigahertz (GHz), 1 billion cycles per second. Typical speeds for a PC are between 2 and 4 GHz. The greater the clock speed, the faster instructions will be executed.

Word length

The word size of a computer is the number of bits that the CPU can process simultaneously. Bits may be grouped into 8-, 16-, 32-, 64- or 128-bit 'words', and processed as a unit during input and output, arithmetic and logic instructions. A processor with a 32-bit word size will operate faster than a processor with a 16-bit word size, and word size is a major factor in determining the speed of a processor. Typical word lengths are 32 or 64 bits.

Address bus and data bus width

Both the addresses of data and instructions, and the data and instructions themselves, are transmitted along buses. The width of the address bus determines the maximum memory address that can be directly referenced. For example, if the width of the address bus is 16 bits, the maximum address that can be transmitted is 11111111 11111111 in binary which is 2^{16} - 1 or 65,535. In all, 65,536 addresses, from 0 to 65,535, can be referenced. In order to send larger addresses, say up to 2^{32} - 1, the address needs to be sent in two groups of 16 bits, which has a detrimental effect on performance. Increasing the width of the address bus would allow more memory locations to be accessed.

The width of the data bus determines how many bits can be transferred simultaneously. This is usually but not always the same as the word size of the computer. Not all processors with a 32-bit word for example have a 32-bit data bus, and so the data may have to be fetched in two groups of 16 bits. Increasing the bus size to 32 bits will therefore increase performance.

5-26

The role of interrupts (A Level only)

An **interrupt** is a signal sent by a software program or a hardware device to the CPU. A software interrupt occurs when an application program terminates or requests certain services from the operating system. A hardware interrupt may occur, for example, when an I/O operation is complete or an error such as `Printer out of paper' occurs.

When the CPU receives an interrupt signal, it suspends execution of the running program or process and puts the values of each register and the program counter onto the system stack, while an **Interrupt Service Routine** is called to deal with the interrupt. Depending on the type of interrupt, a particular routine will be run in order to service it. Once the interrupt has been serviced, the original values of the registers are retrieved from the stack and the fetch-execute cycle resumes from the point that it left off. A test for the presence of interrupts is carried out at the end of each instruction cycle.

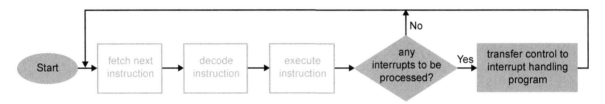

Exercises

1. (a) State the full names of two of the special purpose registers that are used in the fetch part of the fetch-execute cycle.

   Register 1 ....

   Register 2 .... [2]

   (b) Figure 1 below is an incomplete diagram of the fetch-execute cycle.

   Describe the missing steps 1, 2b and 4 using either register transfer notation or written description. Steps 2a and 2b occur at the same time.

   Figure 1

   Step 1 ....

   ....

   Step 2a: PC ← [PC] + 1

   Step 2b ....

   Step 3: CIR ← [MBR]

   Step 4 ....

   Step 5: Execute Instruction

   [3]

   AQA Comp 2 Qu 2 June 2013

Exercises continued

2. **Figure 2** below shows an incomplete diagram of the components of a processor.

Figure 2

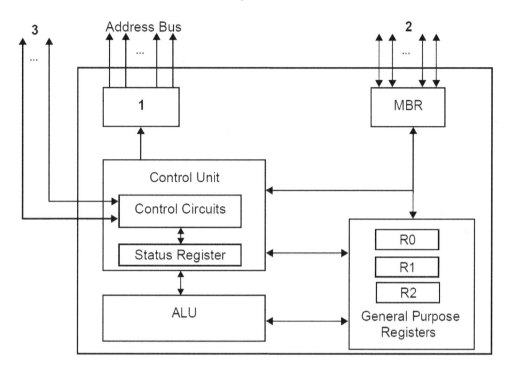

(a) Provide full names for the components numbered 1 to 3 in Figure 2 by completing the table below.

Component number	Component name
1	
2	
3	

[3]

(b) What is the role of the Control Unit? [1]

(c) State the full name of the processor component that would perform subtraction and comparison operations. [1]

(d) What is meant by the term *register*? [1]

(e) State **one** example of when the status register might have a bit set. [1]

AQA Comp 2 Qu 3 January 2012

5-26

Chapter 27 – The processor instruction set

Objectives

- Understand the term 'processor instruction set'
- Learn that instructions consist of an opcode and one or more operands, where an operand could be a value, a memory address or a register
- Understand and apply immediate and direct addressing modes

The processor instruction set

Each different type of processor has its own instruction set, comprising all the instructions which are supported by its hardware. The instruction set of a typical computer includes the following types of instructions:

- **Data transfer** such as LOAD, STORE
- **Arithmetic operations** such as ADD, SUBTRACT
- **Comparison operators** to compare two values
- **Logical operators** – AND, OR, NOT, XOR
- **Branching** – conditional and unconditional
- **Logical** – shift bits right or left
- **Halt**

Format of a machine code instruction

The basic structure of a machine code instruction may take the format shown below:

Operation code		Operand(s)							
Basic machine operation	**Addressing mode**								
0 1 0 0 0 1	0 1	0	0	0	0	0	0	1	1

The number of bits allocated to the **operation code** (opcode) and the **operand** will vary according to the architecture and word size of the particular processor type. The above example shows an instruction held in one 16-bit word. In this particular machine, all operations are assumed to take place in a single register called the **accumulator**.

In more complex architectures, each machine code instruction may occupy up to 32 bits and allow for two operands, for example specifying that:

- a number stored at address 578 is to be loaded into register 3
- the number stored at address 580 is to be added to the contents of register 1
- the number in register 6 is to be stored in address 600

Addressing modes

The operation code (**opcode**) consists of binary digits representing the basic operation such as ADD or LOAD, and a 2-digit code representing the **addressing mode**. We will show examples of just two addressing modes – **immediate** and **direct** addressing. These two addressing modes could be indicated by, for example, 00 or 01 in the two 'addressing mode' bits. (Note that real processors have more than two addressing modes so two or more bits would be required.)

In **immediate addressing**, the operand is the **actual value** to be operated on, say 3 or 75.

In **direct addressing**, the operand holds the **memory address** of the value to be operated on.

Example: Suppose that the operation code 010001, with addressing mode 00, means "Load the operand into the accumulator".

The instruction below with addressing mode 00, in this example meaning **immediate** addressing, will result in the actual value 3 being loaded into the accumulator.

0	1	0	0	0	1	0	0	0	0	0	0	0	0	1	1

Q1: Suppose that the opcode 010000 means STORE and the addressing mode 01 indicates direct addressing.

Describe the operation that will be performed by the following machine code instruction:
010000 01 00100001

A simple model

In this course, a simple model will be used in which the addressing mode is incorporated into the bits allocated to the opcode. The opcode will therefore define both the basic machine code operation and the addressing mode.

For example, in this model an 8-bit instruction will be represented as follows:

Opcode		Operand
Basic machine operation	**Addressing mode**	
001	0	0110

Assuming that the code 001 means ADD, and addressing mode 0 means immediate addressing, the above instruction means "Add the number 6 to the contents of the accumulator".

Q2: Suppose that the opcode 010 means LOAD and the addressing mode 1 indicates direct addressing.

Describe the operation that will be performed by the following machine code instruction:
0101 1100

Q3: What is the maximum value of the operand that can be represented in 4 bits?

Q4: How many different opcodes incorporating an addressing mode can be represented in 4 bits?

Assembly language instructions

Machine code was the first "language" used to enter programs by early computer programmers. The next advance in programming was to use mnemonics instead of binary codes, and this was called **assembly code** or **assembly language**. Each assembly language instruction translates into one machine code instruction.

Different mnemonic codes are used by different manufacturers, so there are several versions of assembly language.

Typical statements in machine code and assembly language are:

Machine code	Assembly code	Meaning
0100 1100	LDA #12	Load the number 12 into the accumulator
0010 0010	ADD #2	Add the number 2 to the contents of the accumulator
0111 1111	STO 15	Store the result from the accumulator in location 15

The # symbol in this assembly language program signifies that the immediate addressing mode is being used.

Q5: Write a statement in a high level language which performs an operation equivalent to the three statements in the above machine code program, with the result being stored in a location called TOTAL.

Q6: Write a machine code program, and an equivalent assembly language program, to add the contents of locations 10 and 11 and store the result in location 14.

5-27

Exercises

1. A computer with a 16-bit word length uses an instruction set with 6 bits for the opcode, including the addressing mode.

(a) What is an *instruction set*? [1]

(b) How many instructions could be included in the instruction set of this computer? [1]

(c) What is the largest number that can be used as data in the instruction? [1]

(d) What would be the effect of increasing the space allowed for the opcode by 2 bits? [2]

(e) What would be the benefits of increasing the word size of the computer? [2]

2. The high-level language statement

        X = Y + 6

is to be written in assembly language.

Complete the following assembly language statements, which are to be the equivalent of the above high level language statement. The LOAD and STORE instructions imply the use of the accumulator register.

        LOAD ....
        ....#6
        STORE ....   [3]

Exercises continued

3. **Figure 1** and **Figure 2** show different versions of the same program.

Figure 1			Figure 2		
(x)	(y)	(z)	(x)	(y)	(z)
200	LOAD	7	200	01010110	00000111
201	ADD	3	201	11010000	00000011
202	ADD	6	202	11010000	00000110
203	STORE	255	203	11110000	11111111

(a) What type of programming language is shown in Figure 2? [1]

(b) In both figures there is a column labelled **(x)**

What would be a suitable heading for this column? [1]

(c) In both figures the instruction is split into two parts.

What are the names of the instruction parts in columns **(y)** and **(z)**? [2]

(d) What is the relationship between the instructions in **Figure 1** and **Figure 2**? [1]

AQA Comp 2 Qu 4 June 2011

5-27

Chapter 28 – Assembly language

Objectives

- Use basic machine code operations expressed in mnemonic-form assembly language
- Understand and apply immediate and direct addressing modes

Assembly language

Assembly language uses mnemonics to represent the operation codes and addresses. Typically, 2-, 3- or 4-character mnemonics are used to represent all the machine code instructions. The **assembler** then translates the assembly language program into machine code for execution.

The following table shows typical mnemonics for data transfer, arithmetic, branch and compare instructions in the instruction set of a particular computer.

LDR Rd, <memory ref>	Load the value stored in the memory location specified by <memory ref> into register d.
STR Rd, <memory ref>	Store the value that is in register d into the memory location specified by <memory ref>.
ADD Rd, Rn, <operand>	Add the value specified in <operand> to the value in register n and store the result in register d.
SUB Rd, Rn, <operand>	Subtract the value specified by <operand> from the value in register n and store the result in register d.
MOV Rd, <operand>	Copy the value specified by <operand> into register d.
CMP Rn, <operand>	Compare the value stored in register n with the value specified by <operand>.
B <label>	Always branch to the instruction at position <label> in the program.
B<condition> <label>	Conditionally branch to the instruction at position <label> in the program if the last comparison met the criteria specified by the <condition>. Possible values for <condition> and their meaning are: EQ: Equal to, NE: Not equal to, GT: Greater than, LT: Less than.
HALT	Stops the execution of the program.

Table 1

<operand> can be interpreted in two different ways, depending on whether the first symbol is a # or an R:

- # – use the decimal value specified after the #, e.g. #27 means use the decimal number 27
- Rn – use the value stored in register n, e.g. R6 means use the value stored in register 6.
- Assume the available registers that the programmer can use are numbered 0 to 7.

Q1: Write two instructions to

(i) compare the value held in register 1 with the integer 100.

(ii) branch to the instruction labelled .loop1 if register 1 does not contain 100.

Examples

All the examples below use instructions from Table 1.

Data transfer and arithmetic operations

Add 12 to the number stored in memory location 52 and save the result in memory location 53.

```
LDR R0, 52        ;Load the contents of location 52 into R0
ADD R0, R0, #12   ;Add 12 to R0
STR R0, 53        ;Store the result in location 53
```

Compare and branch instructions

The value in a memory location can be compared with the value in a register using a CMP (compare) instruction. The code can then be made to conditionally branch to a given label in the program depending on whether the number held in the register was Equal to (BEQ), Not Equal to (BNE), Greater Than (BGT) or Less Than (BLT) the number held in the memory location.

Example: Compare the two numbers held in memory locations 35 and 40. If the value in location 35 is greater than the value in location 40, branch to the instruction labelled `next`, where the program will halt.

```
        LDR R1, 35
        LDR R2, 40
        CMP R1, R2
        BGT next
        ...
        ...
next:   HALT
```

Example: Write the assembly language equivalent of the following high-level language instructions, explaining each assembly language instruction used.

```
A ← 0
repeat
  A ← A + 1
until A = 99
```

Assembly language code:

```
      MOV R0, #0      ;Load the initial value of A into Register 0
loop:
      ADD R0, R0, #1  ;Add 1 to Register 0
      CMP R0, #99     ;Compare R0 with the value 99
      BNE loop        ;Branch if not equal to label loop.
```

> **Q2:** Register 1 holds the value 200 in the 8-bit operand. The format of the ADD instruction is:
>
> | ADD Rd, Rn, <operand> | Add the value specified in <operand> to the value in register n and store the result in register d. |
> |---|---|
>
> What will be the bit pattern held in R2 after execution of the following statement?
>
> ADD R2, R1, 64
>
> What other register will be changed? (Hint: Look back at the **dedicated registers** on page 133.)

5-28

Logical bitwise operators

Assembly language instructions for logical operations are shown in Table 2 below.

`AND Rd, Rn, <operand>`	Perform a bitwise logical AND operation between the value in register n and the value specified by `<operand>` and store the result in register d.
`ORR Rd, Rn, <operand>`	Perform a bitwise logical OR operation between the value in register n and the value specified by `<operand>` and store the result in register d.
`EOR Rd, Rn, <operand>`	Perform a bitwise logical exclusive or (XOR) operation between the value in register n and the value specified by `<operand>` and store the result in register d.
`MVN Rd, <operand>`	Perform a bitwise logical NOT operation on the value specified by `<operand>` and store the result in register d.
`LSL Rd, Rn, <operand>`	Logically shift left the value stored in register n by the number of bits specified by `<operand>` and store the result in register d.
`LSR Rd, Rn, <operand>`	Logically shift right the value stored in register n by the number of bits specified by `<operand>` and store the result in register d.
`HALT`	Stop the execution of the program.

Table 2

The instructions OR, NOT, AND and XOR (exclusive OR) produce the following results:

		OR	NOT	AND	XOR
Inputs	A	1010	1010	1010	1010
	B	1100		1100	1100
Result		1110	0101	1000	0110

The NOT function can be used to find the two's complement of a number:

A	0110 0111
NOT A	1001 1000
Add 1	1
2's complement	1001 1001

The assembly language instructions to carry out this operation with B indicating a binary, rather than a decimal value, would be something like:

```
MVN R1, #01100111B    ;perform NOT operation, store result in R1
ADD R1, R1, #1        ;add 1 to result in R1
```

The OR function can be used to set certain bits to 1 without affecting the other bits in the binary code. For example, a system has eight lights that can be turned on (output 1) or off (output 0), controlled by an 8-bit binary code. At present, lights 1 to 4 are on. We now wish to turn on lights 5 and 7 as well.

Light numbers	1	2	3	4	5	6	7	8
Present output	1	1	1	1	0	0	0	0
OR with	0	0	0	0	1	0	1	0
Result	1	1	1	1	1	0	1	0

5-28

The assembly language code for this operation could be:

```
LDR R2, LIGHT              ;load contents of LIGHT into R2
ORR R3, R2, #00001010B     ;OR with binary 00001010 and store in R3
STR R3, LIGHT              ;Store result back in LIGHT
```

The AND function can be used to mask out certain bits of a number. For example, if we input the ASCII character 3 at the keyboard, the ASCII pattern 00110011 is input. In order to change this to a pure binary digit, we need to mask out the first 4 bits.

```
LDR R2, NUM                ;load ASCII digit from NUM into R2
AND R3, R2, #00001111B     ;AND with binary 00001111 and store in R3
STR R3, NUM                ;Store result back in NUM
```

Q3: Write an instruction to clear bit 2 in register 3 and store the result in register 4.
(Bit 2 is the second bit from the left.)

Logical shift operations

A logical shift right causes the least significant bit to be shifted into the **carry** bit and a zero moves in to occupy the vacated space.

Suppose R1 contained the following bit pattern:

| 0 | 1 | 0 | 0 | 0 | 1 | 1 | 1 | | 0 | (carry bit) |

After the instruction

```
LSR R2, R1, #1        ;Logically shift right the value in R1 by 1 place, store in R2
```
R2 will hold the bit pattern

| 0 | 0 | 1 | 0 | 0 | 0 | 1 | 1 | | 1 |

This can be used for examining the least significant bit of a number. After the operation, the carry bit can be tested and a conditional branch instruction executed.

Q4: Where is the carry bit to be found? (Hint: Look back at the **dedicated registers** on page 133.)

Q5: Register 2 holds the following bit pattern.

| 0 | 1 | 0 | 1 | 0 | 0 | 1 | 1 |

What will be the contents of R2 and R3 after execution of the following instruction?
```
LSL R3, R2, #3        ; (add a description of the instruction here)
```

145

Exercises

1. Memory locations FIRST, SECOND and THIRD each contain an integer. With the aid of the following trace table, explain what the following assembly code does.

```
        LDR R0, FIRST
        LDR R1, SECOND
        LDR R2, THIRD
        CMP R0, R1
        BGT label1
        LDR R0, SECOND
label1:
        CMP R0, R2
        BGT label2
        LDR R0, THIRD
label2:
        STR R0, M
```
[3]

Trace table:

FIRST	SECOND	THIRD	R0	R1	R2	M
17	25	19				

The following mnemonic codes have been used:

LDR Rd, <memory ref>	Load the value stored in the memory location specified by <memory ref> into register d.
STR Rd, <memory ref>	Store the value that is in register d into the memory location specified by <memory ref>.
CMP Rn, <operand>	Compare the value stored in register n with the value specified by <operand>.
B<condition> <label>	Conditionally branch to the instruction at position <label> in the program if the last comparison met the criteria specified by the <condition>. Possible values for <condition> and their meaning are: EQ: Equal to, NE: Not equal to, GT: Greater than, LT: Less than.

2. (a) In a particular machine code, the opcode is stored in 6 bits and the operand is stored in 12 bits. What is the maximum number of operations in the machine's instruction set? [1]

(b) Explain, with the aid of examples, the difference between immediate and direct addressing. [4]

Exercises continued

3. A single accumulator microprocessor supports the assembly language instructions:

```
LOAD    memory reference
ADD     memory reference
STORE   memory reference
```

An example instruction is:

```
LOAD 4
```

which would copy the contents of the referenced memory location 4 into the accumulator register.

(a) (i) Identify which part of the instruction is the *operand* and which part is the *opcode* by writing the words operand and opcode in the two boxes below.

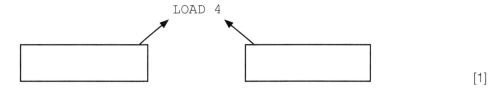

[1]

(ii) The accumulator is a general purpose register.

What is a *register*?   [1]

(b) Using the assembly language instructions, write an assembly language program that adds together the values stored in memory locations 12 and 13, storing the resulting total in memory location 14.   [3]

AQA Comp 2 Qu 5 January 2010

5-28

4. A process can only begin if bits 0, 3, 5 and 6 of an 8-bit accumulator are set to 1. The status of the other bits has no effect on the process. Write the key assembly language instructions to check whether the process can take place.   [3]

Chapter 29 – Input-output devices

Objectives

- Learn the main characteristics and principles of operation of:
  - Barcode reader
  - Digital camera
  - Laser printer
  - RFID
- Understand the purposes and suitability of these devices

Barcodes

Barcodes first started appearing on grocery items in the 1970s, and today, they are used for identification in thousands of applications from tracking parcels, shipping cartons, passenger luggage, blood, tissue and organ products around the world to the sale of items in shops and the recording of the details of people attending events.

A handheld barcode scanner used for scanning medical samples

There are two different types of barcode: Linear barcodes such as the one shown above and 2D barcodes such as the **Quick Response (QR)** code, which can hold more information than the 1D barcode.

A 2D barcode

2D barcodes are used for example in ticketless entry to concerts, or access through gates to board a Eurostar train or passenger airline. They are also used in mobile phone apps which enable the user to take a photo of the code which may then provide them with further information such as a map of their location, product details or a website URL.

Barcode readers

There are four different barcode readers available, each using a slightly different technology for reading and decoding a barcode. The four types are pen-type readers, laser scanners, CCD readers and camera-based readers.

Pen-type readers

In a pen-type reader, a light source and a photo diode are placed next to each other in the tip of a pen. To read a barcode, the tip of the pen is dragged across all the bars at an even speed. The photo diode measures the intensity of the light reflected back from the light source and generates a waveform that is used to measure the widths of the bars and spaces in the barcode. Dark bars in the barcode absorb light and white spaces reflect light so that the voltage waveform generated by the photo diode, once converted from analogue to digtal, is an exact duplicate of the bar and space pattern in the barcode. The simplest encoding translates areas of light and dark as 1s and 0s. These can be used to create ASCII character codes for an alphanumeric string, which may be, for example, a product code or library book number.

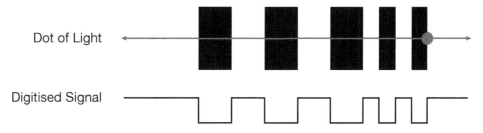

Digital representation of a barcode

5-29

Q1: Using 7-bit the ASCII code on page 73, how would the digital wave pattern above be translated, assuming a black bar equated to a 1 and a white space, a 0?

A pen or wand barcode scanner

Because of their simple design, the pen-type scanner is the most durable type of barcode scanner, and can be tightly sealed against dust, dirt, and other environmental hazards. However, their applications are limited because they must come into direct contact with a barcode to read it.

Because of their small size and low weight, this type of barcode scanner is ideally suited for use with portable (laptop) computers or very low volume scanning applications.

Laser scanners

Laser scanners work in the same way as pen scanners except they use a laser beam as the light source. The laser reflects off a moving mirror which allows the barcode to be read in many different positions. They are available in a variety of forms, the most familiar being the in-counter units in supermarkets. They are reliable and economical for low-volume applications.

Laser scanner

CCD (Charge-Coupled Device) readers

CCD readers use an array of hundreds of tiny light sensors lined up in a row in the head of the reader. Each sensor measures the intensity of the light immediately in front of it. Each individual light sensor in the CCD reader is extremely small and because there are hundreds of sensors lined up in a row, a voltage pattern identical to the pattern in a barcode is generated in the reader by sequentially measuring the voltages across each sensor in the row.

Camera-based readers

A camera-based **imaging scanner** uses a camera and image processing techniques to decode a 1D or 2D bar code. An imaging scanner can read a barcode on any surface, printed or onscreen, and can also read a code that is damaged or poorly printed. Image processing has to be carried out by the software as the barcode might be at any rotation or variety of distances from the scanner. They are used in multiple applications such as:

- age verification by scanning an individual's driving licence

- couponing – a 2D barcode coupon is emailed to a customer, which can be scanned from their phone screen at the POS (Point of Sale). Unique codes for each customer and promotion can be stored in the bar code, so that tracking coupon usage is easy

- event ticketing – tickets can be issued electronically and then scanned off a phone screen

Consumers can use a cell phone to scan a QR code which can, for example:

- display a catalogue of movies or DVDs

- play an MP3 when scanned

- display nutrition information about a product

Digital cameras

A digital camera uses a **CCD** or **CMOS** (Complementary Metal Oxide Semiconductor) sensor comprising millions of tiny light sensors arranged in a grid. When the shutter opens, light enters the camera and projects an 'image' onto the sensor at the back of the lens. Like the CCD barcode reader, each sensor measures the brightness of each pixel, turns light into electricity and stores the amount of charge as binary data. The image on the camera's screen is a greyscale representation of what the sensors are 'seeing'. To record colour, the sensors are often placed under a mosaic of red, green and blue filters to separate out the different colour wavelengths. The processor can then approximate binary values for the three RGB channels of each individual pixel based on the values of neighbouring pixels. The binary data is recorded onto the camera's memory card so that the image can be reproduced using suitable software.

A CCD sensor tends to produce higher quality images and they are used in higher end cameras. They are also more reliable since the technology has been around for much longer. This however, is at the cost of power consumption, using up to 100 times that of a CMOS sensor.

> **Q2:** Suggest a suitable sensor type for use in a mobile phone camera and give a reason why.

Bayer colour filter applied to a sensor array

Radio Frequency Identification (RFID)

In much the same way as barcodes, RFID tags are increasingly being used to identify and track everything from household products and cars to bank cards and animals. The difference however, is that an RFID tag can be read without line of sight and from up to 300 metres away. They can also pass stored data from the tag to the receiver and vice versa. An RFID chip consists of a small microchip transponder and an antenna. The microchip at the centre of the image below can be manufactured to be less than 1mm in size but the antenna must be larger in order for it to communicate with a base unit. This can increase the size of the smallest tags to about that of a large grain of rice. These can be embedded in special capsules and injected under the skin for the identification of pets.

5-29

Passive and active tags

Active tags are physically larger as they include a battery to power the tag so that it actively transmits a signal for a reader to pick up. These are used to track things likely to be read from further away, such as cars as they pass through a motorway toll booth or runners in a marathon as they pass mile markers. Passive tags are much cheaper to produce as they do not have a battery. They rely on the radio waves emitted from a reader up to a metre away to provide sufficient electromagnetic power to the card using its coiled antenna. Once energised, the transponder inside the RFID tag can send its data to the reader nearby. These are most common in tagging items such as some groceries, music CDs, and for smart cards such as Transport for London's Oyster Card or a contactless bank card.

Laser printer

Laser printers offer high-quality, high-speed printing. Their function is similar to that of a photocopier, using powdered ink called toner. The printer generates a bitmap image of the printed page and using a laser unit and mirror, 'draws' a negative, reverse image onto a negatively charged drum. The laser light causes the affected areas of the drum to lose their charge. The drum then rotates past a toner hopper to attract charged toner particles onto the areas which have not been lasered. The particles are transferred onto a sheet of paper and then bonded onto it using pressure and heat.

Laser printers are becoming increasingly affordable and are frequently used as home printers, in businesses and in professional printing services. Colour laser printers are far more expensive to run than black and white versions. They contain four toner cartridges (Cyan, Magenta, Yellow and Black or CMYK) and the paper must go through a similar process to the black-only printer four times; once for each colour. The usage of laser printers for print jobs other than text is limited by the quality of the print produced, which at about 1200 dpi makes photorealistic prints impossible and best left to inkjet printers.

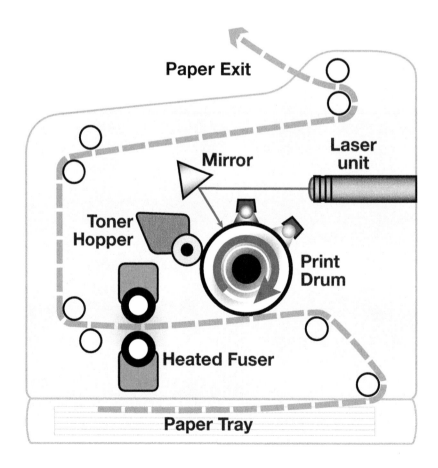

Exercises

1. A supermarket uses a computerised stock control system. Each product is identified by a unique product code which is printed on the product as a bar code. The bar codes are input into the stock control system at the till using a bar code reader. One of the digits in the bar code is a check digit.

   (a) Describe the principles of operation of a bar code reader, **excluding** the use of the check digit. [4]

   (b) Explain the purpose of the check digit. [1]

   (c) Some unpackaged items such as loose fruit and vegetables do not have a product code printed on them.

   Name an input device that the till operator could use to enter details of these items. [1]

   AQA Comp 2 Qu 9 January 2010

2. A Radio Frequency Identification (RFID) system is made up of a transponder built into an RFID tag and an interrogator or reader. One example of use is to detect unauthorised removal of library books from a library.

   Explain the principles of operation of this RFID system. [2]

   AQA Comp 2 Qu 11 January 2009

3. Some countries have introduced electronic passports for their citizens. The passport stores data about the passport holder using a Radio Frequency Identification (RFID) tag.

   Explain how the RFID tag could be read at passport control in an airport. [2]

5-29

Chapter 30 – Storage devices

Objectives

- Explain the need for secondary storage within a computer system
- Know the main characteristics and principles of operations of:
  - Hard disk
  - Optical disk
  - Solid-state disk (SSD)
- Understand the purposes and suitability of these devices

The need for secondary storage

A computer's primary store is Random Access Memory. Unlike RAM, secondary storage is not directly accessible to the processor and has slower access speeds. Secondary storage, however, has the advantage that it retains its contents when the computer's power is turned off. This includes the computer's internal hard disk, optical media and solid state disks.

How storage devices store data

Hard disks, optical disks and solid state disks all use different methods to store data, but in each case, use a technique which allows them to create and maintain a toggle state without power to represent either a 1 or a 0.

Hard disk

A hard disk uses rigid rotating platters coated with magnetic material. Ferrous (iron) particles on the disk are polarised to become either a north or south state. This represents 0 and 1. The disk is divided into tracks in concentric circles, and each track is subdivided into sectors. The disk spins very quickly at speeds of up to 10,000 RPM. Like an old record player, a drive head (like the needle on a record player) moves across the disk to access different tracks and sectors. Data is read or written to the disk as it passes under the drive head. The head, however, is not in contact with the disk, but floats a fraction of a millimetre above it. When the drive head is not in use, it is parked to one side of the disk in order to prevent damage from movement. A hard disk may consist of several platters, each with its own drive head.

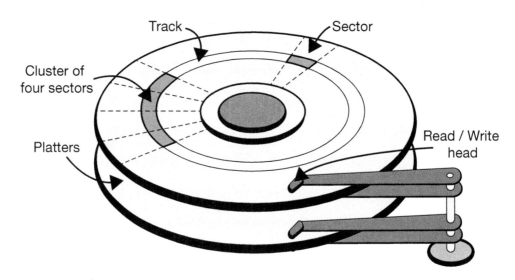

Although hard disks are less portable than optical or solid state media, their huge capacity makes them very suitable for desktop purposes. Smaller, denser surface areas spinning under the read-write heads mean that newer 3.5 inch disks have capacities of up to several terabytes.

Optical disk

Optical disks come in three different formats: read-only (e.g. CD-ROM), recordable (e.g. CD-R) and rewritable (e.g. CD-RW). An **optical** disk works by using a high powered laser to "burn" (change the chemical properties of) sections of its surface, making them less reflective. A laser at a lower power is used to read the disk by shining light onto the surface and a sensor is used to measure the amount of light that is reflected back. A read-only CD-ROM disk pressed during manufacture has pits in its surface. Those areas that have not been pitted, are called lands. At the point where a pit starts or ends, light is scattered and therefore not reflected so well. Reflective and non-reflective areas are read as 1s and 0s. There is only one single track on an optical disk, arranged as a tight spiral.

A **CD-ROM** holds about 650MB of data, whereas a **Blu-Ray** disk (designed to supersede the DVD disk) can hold 50GB. Although these disks do not vary in size, their added capacity is owing to the shorter wavelength in the laser they use. This creates much smaller pits, enabling a greater number to fit in the same space along the track and also means that the track can be more tightly wound, and therefore much longer.

Recordable disks use a reflective layer with a transparent dye coating that becomes less reflective when a spot laser "burns" a spot in the track.

Rewriteable compact disks use a laser and a magnet in order to heat a spot on the disk and then set its state to become a 0 or a 1 using the magnet before it cools again. A **DVD-RW** uses a phase change alloy that can change between amorphous and crystalline states by changing the power of the laser beam.

5-30

Pits and Lands   Spiral track

Optical storage is very cheap to produce and easy to send through the post for distribution purposes. Disks are also used for small backups or for storing music, photographs or films. Disk data can however be corrupted or damaged easily by excessive sunlight or scratches.

Solid-state disk (SSD)

Solid state disks are packaged to look like hard disk drives, rectangular in shape and sized to match industry-standard dimensions for hard drives, typically 2.5 and 3.5 inches.

A 480 GB solid state drive

Inside, however, instead of platters and a read-write head, there is an array of chips arranged on a board. These components are put into the standard size "housing" so that they fit into existing laptops and desktop PCs. Solid state memory comprises millions of **NAND** flash memory cells, and a controller that manages pages and blocks of memory. Each cell works by delivering a current along the bit and word lines to activate the flow of electrons from the source towards the drain. The current on the word line however is strong enough to force a few electrons across an insulated oxide layer into a floating gate. Once the current is turned off, these electrons are trapped. The state of the NAND cell is determined by measuring the charge in the floating gate. No charge (with no electrons) is considered a 1 and some charge is considered a 0.

Data is stored in pages (typically 4KiB each), grouped into blocks of say, 512KiB. NAND flash memory cannot overwrite existing data. The old data must be erased before data can be written to the same location, and although data can be written in pages, the technology requires the whole block to be erased. As writing to a specific block of NAND cells cannot be done directly, a separate block is created to mirror the data to be transferred to the solid state memory and the data is then written to the new block. The contents of the original block are marked as "invalid" or "stale" and are erased when the user wants to write new data to the drive.

Although capacity is still relatively low, solid state media have faster access speed than hard disks. With no need to move a read-write head across the disk, one piece of data can be accessed just as quickly as any other, even if they are not close together.

SSDs consume far less power than traditional hard drives, meaning that in a laptop, for example, battery life is extended and they stay cooler. In addition, they are less susceptible to damage.

They are also silent in operation, lighter and highly portable – all considerable advantages in personal devices such as mobile phones and MP3 players for example.

Q1: Look up some specifications and prices for hard drives and SSDs.

Exercises

1. (a) Describe how data is written to and read from a CD-R disk. [3]

(b) A school has archived all its students' reports on to CD-R. Some years later, a copy of a particular student's reports is requested. Unfortunately it is found that the documents cannot be opened.

Give **two** reasons why this may be the case. [2]

2. In 1995, a high capacity hard disk drive had a storage capacity of 512 mebibytes. In 2012, a typical hard disk drive of the same physical size had a capacity of 1 tebibyte.

(a) Describe the principles of operation of a hard disk drive. [4]

(b) How many times greater is the storage capacity of a 1 tebibyte hard disk drive than that of a 512 mebibyte hard disk drive?

Show each stage of your working. [1]

Final answer: _____ [1]

(c) Give **one** development in the design of hard disk drives that has enabled this increase in storage capacity. [1]

(d) If you are considering purchasing a high-end desktop or laptop you might be offered the option of a solid-state drive (SSD) rather than a traditional hard disk drive.

A solid-state drive is a data storage device that uses solid-state memory, similar to that in USB flash drives (memory sticks), to store data that is accessed in a similar way to a traditional hard disk drive.

Ignoring any differences in price and assuming that both drives have the same capacity, state **two** reasons why you might choose the solid-state drive. [2]

AQA Comp 2 Qu 5 January 2013

5-30

Section 6

Communication: technology and consequences

In this section:

6

Chapter 31 – Communication methods

Objectives

- Define serial and parallel transmission methods and discuss the advantages of serial over parallel transmission

- Define and compare synchronous and asynchronous data transmission

- Describe the purpose of start and stop bits in asynchronous data transmission

- Define baud rate, bit rate, bandwidth, latency, protocol

- Differentiate between baud rate and bit rate

- Understand the relationship between bit rate and bandwidth

Electronic data communication

Data communication involves sending and receiving data from one computer or device to another. Data communication applications include e-mail, supermarket EPOS (electronic point of sale) terminals, cash dispensers, cell phones and VOIP (Voice Over Internet Protocol).

Data communication also takes place within the CPU and between the CPU and its peripheral devices; for example, data and addresses are transmitted along the data bus and address bus between the processor and memory, and data is transferred between memory and storage and other peripheral devices.

Serial and parallel data communication

Data can be sent in one of two ways: serial or parallel.

Using **serial data transmission**, bits are sent via an interface one bit at a time over a single wire from the source to the destination. Very high data transfer rates can be achieved – for example using fibre-optic cable, data transfer rates ranging from around 50 Megabits per second (Mbs) to 100 Gigabits per second (Gbs) can be achieved.

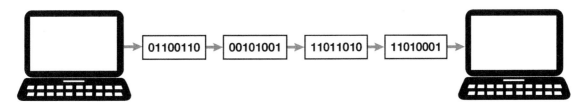

Serial transmission

Using **parallel data transmission**, several bits are sent simultaneously over a number of parallel wires.

Parallel communication is used in integrated circuits and within random access memory (RAM).

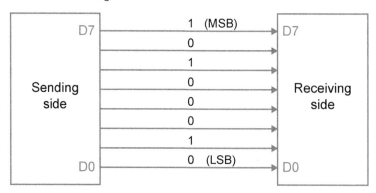

Parallel transmission

When parallel transmission is used, each individual wire has slightly different properties, there is a possibility that bits could travel at slightly different speeds over each of the wires. This produces a problem known as skew. Parallel transmission is only reliable over short distances.

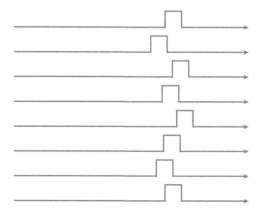

Skew developing in parallel wires

Advantages of serial over parallel transmission

The advantages of serial over parallel links are summarised below.

- The significant reduction in the size and complexity of connectors in serial transmission results in much lower associated costs. Designers of devices such as smartphones use connectors that are small, durable and still produce acceptable performance.

- "Crosstalk" creates interference between parallel lines, and can result in corrupted words which then need to be retransmitted. This is more pronounced as the signal frequency increases, and worsens with the length of the communication link.

- Serial links are reliable over much greater distances than parallel links.

- Because of the lack of interference at higher frequencies, signal frequency can be much higher with serial transmission, resulting in a higher net data transfer rate even though less data is transmitted per cycle. (See bit rate and baud rate below.)

6-31

Bit rate and baud rate

The speed at which data is transmitted serially is measured in bits per second (**bit rate**). The **baud rate** is the rate at which the signal changes.

In baseband mode, only two voltage levels are most commonly used, one to represent zero and the other to represent one. In this case the bit rate and the baud rate are the same.

bit rate of channel = (baud rate) x (number of bits per signal)

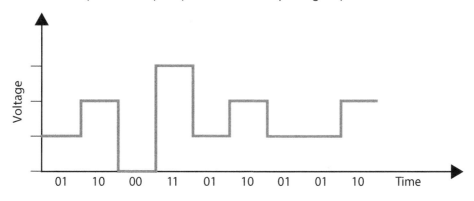

One signal encoding 2 bits: bit rate is twice the baud rate

In the figure above, (a simplified version of reality), four different "voltage levels" on the vertical scale represent four different bit patterns, so 00, 01, 10 or 11 can be encoded at each signal.

With eight different voltage levels or frequencies, each signal can encode 3 bits. Thus, for example, a baud rate of 1 MBd (megabaud) = 3 Mbit/s or 3,000,000 bits per second.

Bandwidth

Bandwidth is the range of frequencies that a transmission medium can carry. The larger the range, the greater the amount of data that can be transmitted in a fixed amount of time. It is usually expressed in bits per second (bps), since **there is a direct relationship between bandwidth and bit rate**. Think of a pipe carrying water – the larger the width of the pipe, the more water can be sent along it.

Modern networks typically have speeds measured in millions of bits per second (Mbps).

Q1: Carry out a speed test on your PC. (Try http://www.speedtest.net/) Why is the upload speed different from the download speed?

Latency

Latency is the time delay between the moment that transmission of the first byte or packet of a communication starts and when it is received at its destination. It is primarily a function of how long it takes information to travel from source to destination.

When satellite links are involved, the distance travelled can be more than 100,000 kilometers, and the result is often seen on live TV when a presenter in a studio talks to a reporter in a distant place.

6-31

Parity

Computers use either even or odd parity. In an even parity machine, the total number of 'on' bits in every byte (including the parity bit) must be an even number. When data is transmitted, the parity bit is set at the transmitting end and parity is checked at the receiving end, and if the wrong number of bits are 'on', an error has occurred. In the diagram below the parity bit is the most significant bit (MSB).

Parity bit in even parity system

> **Q2:** The ASCII codes for P and Q are 1010000 and 1010001 respectively. In an even parity transmission system, what will be the value of the parity bit for the characters P and Q?

Synchronous transmission

Using **synchronous transmission**, data is transferred at regular intervals that are timed by a clocking signal, allowing for a constant and reliable transmission for time-sensitive data, such as real-time video or voice. Parallel communication typically uses synchronous transmission – for example, in the CPU, the clock emits a signal at regular intervals and transmissions along the address bus, data bus and control bus start on a clock signal, which is shared by both sender and receiver.

Asynchronous transmission

Using **asynchronous transmission**, one byte at a time is sent, with each character being preceded by a start bit and followed by a stop bit.

The start bit alerts the receiving device and synchronises the clock inside the receiver ready to receive the character. The baud rate at the receiving end has to be set up to be the same as the sender's baud rate or the signal will not be received correctly. The stop bit is actually a "stop period", which may be arbitrarily long. This allows the receiver time to identify the next start bit and gives the receiver time to process the data before the next value is transmitted.

A parity bit is also usually included as a check against incorrect transmission. Thus for each character being sent, a total of 10 bits is transmitted, including the parity bit, a start bit and a stop bit. The start bit may be a 0 or a 1, the stop bit is then a 1 or a 0 (always different). A series of electrical pulses is sent down the line as illustrated below:

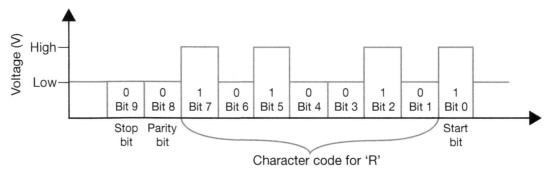

Asynchronous transmission

This type of transmission is usually used by PCs, and is economical for relatively small amounts of data. The main advantage is that there does not need to be a way of sharing the clock signal.

Protocol

Protocol: a set of rules relating to communication between devices.

In order to allow equipment from different suppliers to be networked, a standardised set of rules (protocols) has been devised covering standards for physical connections, cabling, mode of transmission, speed, data format, error detection and correction. Any pieces of equipment which use the same communication protocol can be linked together.

Exercises

1. Data is being transmitted along a serial link using asynchronous data transmission and odd parity.

   (a) Explain what *serial data transmission* is and how it differs from *parallel data transmission*. [2]

   (b) The figure below shows a byte of data being transmitted along the serial link using odd parity.

   Write the missing values of the Stop bit, Parity bit and Start bit on the figure.

		1	0	0	1	1	0	0	
Stop bit	Parity bit	Byte of data							Start bit

   Direction of data transmission [2]

   (c) Explain what asynchronous data transmission is. [1]

   AQA Comp 3 Qu 3 June 2013

2. (a) Explain the terms *bit rate* and *baud rate* and the relationship between the two. [3]

   (b) What is *latency* in the context of data communications? [2]

3. (a) What is meant by a *communications protocol*? [1]

   (b) Why is a communications protocol necessary when communicating over a network? [1]

   (c) Name **five** items that are commonly covered by a communications protocol. [5]

6-31

Chapter 32 – Network topology

Objectives

- Describe the star and bus topologies for a local area network
- Differentiate between physical and logical network topologies
- Explain the operation of these network topologies
- Give the advantages and disadvantages of each

Local area networks

A local area network (LAN) consists of a number of computing devices on a single site or in a single building, connected together by cables. The network may consist of a number of PCs, other devices such as printers and scanners, and a central server. Users on the network can communicate with each other, as well as sharing data and hardware devices such as printers and scanners.

LANs can transmit data very fast but only over a short distance.

Physical bus topology

A LAN can use different layouts or topologies. In a **bus** topology, all computers are connected to a single cable. The ends of the cable are plugged into a terminator.

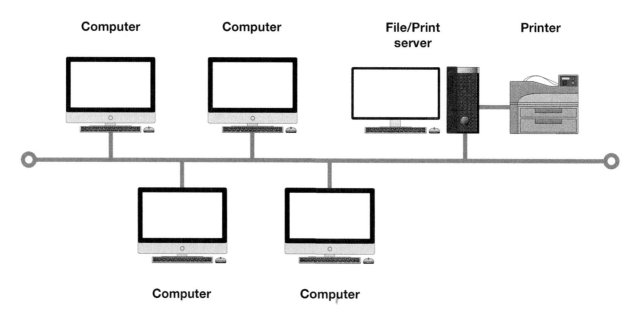

Advantage of a bus topology

- Inexpensive to install as it requires less cable than a star topology and does not require any additional hardware

6-32

Disadvantages of a bus topology

- If the main cable fails, network data can no longer be transmitted to any of the nodes
- Performance degrades with heavy traffic
- Low security – all computers on the network can see all data transmissions

Physical star topology

A **star** network has a central node, which may be a switch or computer which acts as a router to transmit messages.

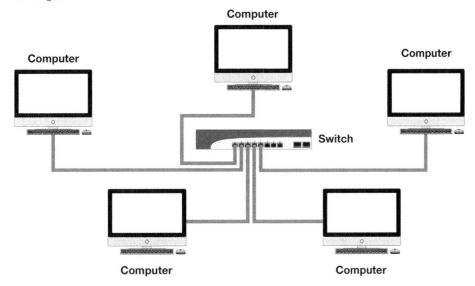

Advantages of a star topology

- If one cable fails, only one station is affected, so it is simple to isolate faults
- Consistent performance even when the network is being heavily used
- Higher transmission speeds can give better performance than a bus network
- No problems with 'collisions' of data since each station has its own cable to the server
- The system is more secure as messages are sent directly to the central computer and cannot be intercepted by other stations
- Easy to add new stations without disrupting the network

Disadvantages of a star network

- May be costly to install because of the length of cable required
- If the central device goes down, network data can no longer be transmitted to any of the nodes

Operation of a star network

In a star network, each node is connected to a central device, typically a switch. A switch keeps a record of the unique MAC address of each device on the network and can identify which particular computer on the network it should send the data to.

6-32

Physical vs logical topology

The **physical** topology of a network is its actual design layout, which is important when you select a wiring scheme and design the wiring for a new network.

The **logical** topology is the shape of the path the data travels in, and describes how components communicate across the physical topology. The physical and logical topologies are independent of each other, so that a network physically wired in star topology can behave logically as a bus network by using a bus protocol and appropriate physical switching.

For example, any variety of Ethernet uses a logical bus topology when components communicate, regardless of the physical layout of the cable.

6-32

In the diagram, the computers on the left are connected with a single cable coming from the switch, in a physical bus configuration. The computers on the right hand side are each separately connected to the switch, in a physical star configuration. Logically, however, the network on the right can be arranged as a bus network and data will be sent to each computer in turn, as on the left. Each individual cable between the switch and the device will act as a bus and the Ethernet bus protocol will be used to control access to the cable, even though there are only two devices (the switch and the device at the other end of the individual cable) which could attempt to put data onto the cable simultaneously.

Operation of a logical bus network

Data cannot be simultaneously transmitted in both directions, i.e. duplex transmission is not possible. Every station receives all network traffic, and the traffic generated by each station has equal transmission priority. A device wanting to communicate with another device on the network sends a broadcast message onto the wire that all other devices see, but only the intended recipient actually accepts and processes the message. **Carrier Sense Multiple Access (CSMA/CD)** technology is used to enable nodes to transmit on the same cable.

Carrier Sense Multiple Access with Collision Detection (CSMA/CD)

If two nodes try to transmit simultaneously, a carrier sensing scheme detects other signals while transmitting a frame. Both nodes then stop transmitting and wait for a random time before trying to re-transmit. **CSMA/CA** (Carrier Sense Multiple Access with Collision Avoidance) is used on wireless networks and is covered in Chapter 34, page 173.

MAC address

Every computer device, whether it's a PC, smartphone, laptop, printer or other device which is capable of being part of a network, must have a **Network Interface Card (NIC)**. Each NIC has a unique **Media Access Control address (MAC address)**, which is assigned and hard-coded into the card by the manufacturer and which uniquely identifies the device. The address is 48 bits long, and is written as 12 hex digits, for example:

00-09-5D-E3-F7-62

Because they are unique, MAC addresses can be used to track you. When you walk around, your smartphone scans for nearby Wi-Fi networks and broadcasts its MAC address.

> **Q1:** A company named Renew London used rubbish bins in the City of London with Wi-Fi monitoring equipment installed in them to track people's movements around the city. What are the implications for personal privacy of such capabilities? How could advertisers use tracking information? Who else might use it?

You can find out the MAC address of your PC by selecting **Command Prompt** from the **Start** menu in Windows, and then typing `ipconfig /all`. This will display the physical address, i.e. MAC address.

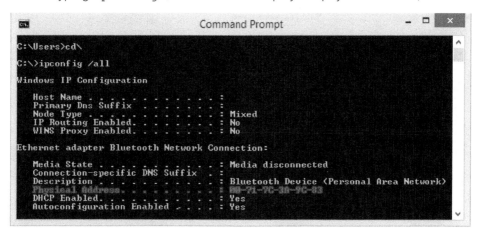

Displaying your computer's MAC address

> **Q2:** Do some research to find out whether you can change the MAC address of your PC. Why might someone want to do this?

Exercises

1. (a) Draw diagrams representing physical **star** and **bus** topologies. [4]

   (b) Describe **three** advantages of a physical star topology over a bus topology, and **one** disadvantage of the star topology. [4]

   (c) Describe how a network wired in a star topology can behave logically as a bus network. [2]

2. A student claims that "an individual piece of hardware may be tracked and identified by its MAC address".

   (a) What is a MAC address? [1]

   (b) Explain briefly how a MAC address is used and state whether you agree with the statement above. [3]

Chapter 33 – Client-server and peer-to-peer

Objectives

- Explain client-server networking

- Explain peer-to-peer networking

- Describe situations when each of these might be used

Client-server networking

In a client-server network, one or more computers known as **clients** are connected to a powerful central computer known as the **server**. Each client may hold some of its own files and resources such as software, and can also access resources held by the server. In a large network, there may be several servers, each performing a different task.

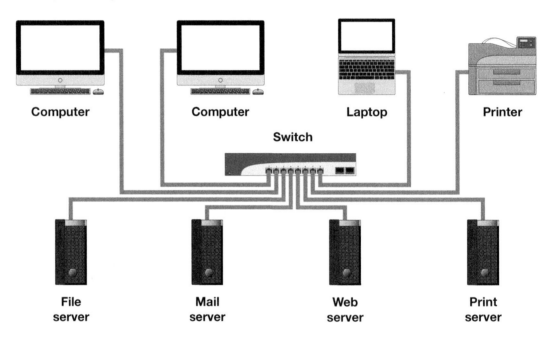

- File server holds and manages data for all the clients

- Print server manages print requests

- Web server manages requests to access the Web

- Mail server manages the email system

- Database server manages database applications

In a client-server network, the client makes a request to the server which then processes the request.

Advantages of a client-server network

- Security is better, since all files are stored in a central location and access rights are managed by the server

- Backups are done centrally so there is no need for individual users to back up their data. If there is a breakdown and some data is lost, recovery procedures will enable it to be restored

- Data and other resources can be shared

Disadvantages of a client-server network

- It is expensive to install and manage

- Professional IT staff are needed to maintain the servers and run the network

Peer-to-peer networks

In a peer-to-peer network, there is no central server. Individual computers are connected to each other, either locally or over a wide area network so that they can share files. In a small local area network, such as in a home or small office, a peer-to-peer network is a good choice because:

- it is cheap to set up

- it enables users to share resources such as a printer or router

- it is not difficult to maintain

Peer-to-peer networks are also used by companies providing, for example, video on demand. The problem arises when thousands of people simultaneously want to download the latest episode of a particular TV show. Using a peer-to-peer network, hundreds of computers can be used to hold parts of the video and so share the load.

6-33

The downside of peer-to-peer networking

Peer-to-peer networking has been widely used for online piracy, since it is impossible to trace the files which are being illegally downloaded. In 2011, the US Chamber of Commerce estimated that piracy sites attracted 53 billion visits each year. The analyst firm *NetNames* estimated that in January 2013 alone, 432 million unique Web users actively searched for content that infringes copyright.

Case study: Piracy sites

In January 1999, 19-year-old Shawn Fanning and Sean Parker created the Napster software, which enabled the peer-to-peer "sharing" of music – in actual fact, the theft of copyright music. Instead of storing the MP3 files on a central computer, the songs are stored on users' machines. When you want to download a song using Napster, you are downloading it from another person's machine, which may be next door or on the other side of the world.

All you need is a copy of the Napster utility and an Internet connection.

Napster was sued for copyright infringement in 2000 but argued that they were not responsible for copyright infringement on other people's machines. However, they lost the case and were pushed into bankruptcy, but the service has since reinvented itself on a legitimate, subscription basis.

How Napster worked

The consequences of piracy

In 2014, Popcorn Time was launched, allowing a decentralised peer-to-peer service for illegal streaming of movies. Popcorn Time has already been translated into 32 languages and has been described as a "nightmare scenario" for the movie industry. The more movies that are stolen and illegally downloaded online, the fewer resources moviemakers have to invest in new films. In 2013 there was a 21% drop in the 18-24 age group buying tickets to watch movies, and numbers may plummet further in the next few years.

A 2011 report by the London-based International Federation of the Phonographic Industry (IFPI) estimated that 1.2 million European jobs would be destroyed by 2015 in the music, movie, publishing and photography industries because of online piracy.

> **Q1:** Look up the **Copyright, Designs and Patents Act 1988**. What types of work are protected by this Act? For what period of time is a work protected by copyright?

Exercises

1. Explain the difference between client-server and peer-to-peer networking, and give an example of where each might be used. [6]

2. Why is it illegal to download music from some Internet sites? [1]

   Describe the consequences to the individual artists and to society as a whole, of online piracy. [5]

Chapter 34 – Wireless networking, CSMA and SSID

Objectives

- Explain the purpose of Wi-Fi
- Describe the components required for wireless networking
- Explain how wireless networks are secured
- Explain the wireless protocol CSMA/CA
- Describe the purpose of Service Set Identifier (SSID)

Wi-Fi

Wi-Fi is a local area wireless technology that enables you to connect a device such as a PC, smartphone, digital audio player, laptop or tablet computer to a network resource or to the Internet via a **wireless network access point (WAP)**. An access point has a range of about 20 metres indoors, and more outdoors.

Laptop computer   **Wireless access point**   **Printer**

A laptop connected wirelessly to a printer

In 1999, the Wi-Fi Alliance was formed to establish international standards for interoperability and backward compatibility. The Alliance consists of a group of several hundred companies around the world, and enforces the use of standards for device connectivity and network connections.

Components required

In order to connect to a wireless network, a computer device needs a **wireless network adaptor**. The combination of computer and interface controller is called a **station**. All stations share a single radio frequency communication channel, and each station is constantly tuned in on this frequency to pick up transmissions. Transmissions are received by all the stations within range of the wireless access point.

To connect to the Internet, the WAP usually connects to a **router**, but it can also be an integral part of the router itself.

6-34

171

Securing a wireless network

Wi-Fi Protected Access (WPA) and **Wi-Fi Protected Access II (WPA2)**, which has replaced it, are two security protocols and security certification programs used to secure wireless networks. WPA2 is built into wireless network interface cards, and provides strong encryption of data transmissions, with a new 128-bit key being generated for each packet sent.

Each wireless network has a Service Set Identification (SSID) which is the informal name of the local network – for example, HOME-53C1. The purpose of the SSID is to identify the network, and if, for example, you visit someone else's house with a laptop and wish to connect to their Wi-Fi network in order to use the Internet, when you try to log on to the Internet the computer will ask you to enter the name of the network.

Your computer may be within the range of several networks, so having chosen the correct SSID you will then be asked for the password or security key - an identifier of up to 32 bytes, usually a human-readable string. SSIDs must be locally unique.

It is possible to disable the broadcast of your SSID to hide your network from others looking to connect to a named local network. However, this will not hide your network completely.

Whitelists

Some network administrators set up **MAC address whitelists** (the opposite of blacklists) to control who is allowed on their networks. (The MAC address is a unique identifier assigned to a network interface card by the manufacturer: see page 167.)

6-34

Q1: Research some of the applications of "location-based services" such as *Presence Orb*. What are some of the benefits and some of the drawbacks to individuals of tracking software?

Arriva's Bus App

CSMA/CA

CSMA/CA (Carrier Sense Multiple Access/Collision Avoidance) is a protocol for carrier transmission in wireless local area networks.

This protocol attempts to avoid collisions occuring on a data channel, but due to the 'hidden nodes' problem described below, cannot always do so. It has to rely on acknowledgments to know that data has arrived successfully.

Prior to transmitting, a node first listens for signals on the wireless network to determine whether another node is transmitting. If a signal is detected, it waits for a random period of time for the node to stop transmitting and then listens again.

It is still possible that data will collide using this system as two nodes might transmit at the same time as they both sense the channel is idle. This is detected because the receiver would not send an acknowledgment back to the sender that the data is received. RTS/CTS, explained below, is an attempt to overcome this as well as the problem of "hidden nodes".

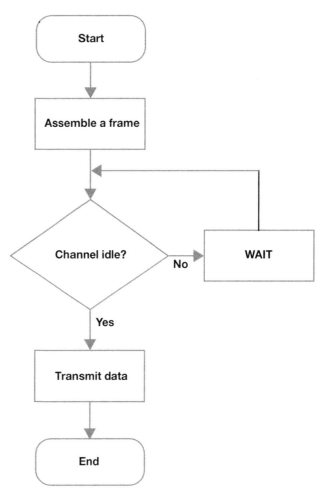

6-34

CSMA/CA with RTS/CTS

Having determined that no other node is transmitting, the station wanting to transmit sends a **Request to Send (RTS)** signal, and the WAP sends a **Clear to Send (CTS)** signal back if and when the channel is idle. This counteracts the problem of "hidden nodes", i.e. a node that can be heard by the WAP but not by the node trying to transmit. This is shown in the figure below, in which nodes A and C can each communicate with the WAP at B, but are hidden from each other.

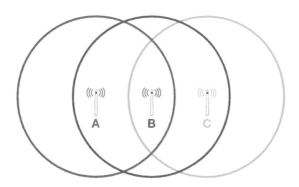

The revised algorithm now looks like this:

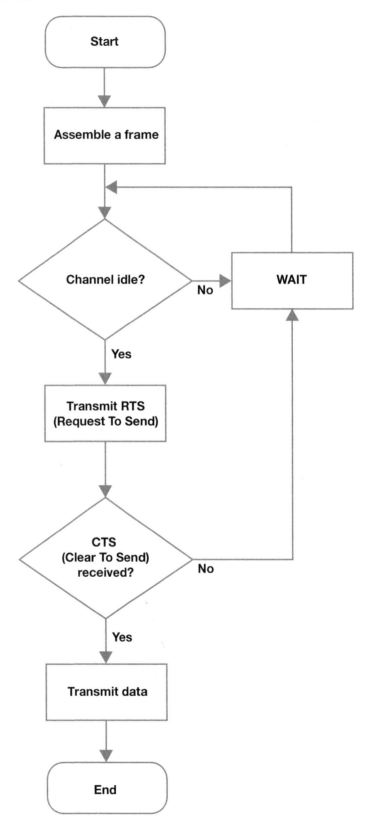

CSMA/CA using RTS/CTS

6-34

Exercises

1. (a) What components are required for wireless networking? [2]

(b) Explain **two** measures that may be taken to make a wireless network secure from hackers. [4]

(c) Explain the **CSMA/CA** with **Request to Send/Clear to Send (RTS/CTS)** protocol. [4]

(d) How does the **RTS/CTS** system reduce the possibility of a data transmission being corrupted? [2]

2. *Wi-Fi location-based technology* is increasingly being used by retailers to maximise sales to potential customers. Describe briefly how this works. What are the benefits of this technology to the retailers and their customers? What are the potential dangers to individuals of widespread use of this technology? [8]

6-34

Chapter 35 – Communication and privacy

Objectives

- To understand that developments in digital technologies have enabled massive transformations in the capacity of organisations to monitor behaviour, amass and analyse personal information

- To understand the issue of scale, and the potential for individual computer scientists and software engineers to produce great good, but also great harm

- Discuss the challenges facing legislators in the digital age

Case Study 1: Edward Snowden

In April 2013, Guardian journalist Glen Greenwald and Academy Award-winning documentary film director and producer Laura Poitras met in the Marriott Hotel in New York to discuss an initial contact with an anonymous "whistle-blower". Seated in the hotel restaurant, Laura Poitras asked Glenn to either remove the battery from his cell phone or leave it in the hotel room. "It sounds paranoid," she said, "but the government has the capability to activate cell phones and laptops remotely as eavesdropping devices. Turning off the phone or laptop does not defeat the capability; only removing the battery does."

The anonymous source had refused to email any details of what material he had to offer until Glenn installed PGP on his computer. PGP, which stands for "Pretty Good Privacy" is a sophisticated tool to prevent online communications from being hacked. The encryption codes are so lengthy and random that it would take years to decrypt a communication. But it was complicated to install and it took Glenn several months to get round to it, before he was eventually talked through the process online by his anonymous contact. Only then did he receive information from his source about a program called PRISM, which allowed America's National Security Agency (NSA) to collect private communications from the world's largest Internet companies, including Facebook, Google, Yahoo, Microsoft, Apple, YouTube, AOL and Skype.

The first document that Glenn opened was a training manual to teach analysts about the new surveillance capabilities. It told analysts how they could query, for example, particular email addresses or telephone numbers and what data they would receive in response.

What did the source hope to achieve by exposing the secret surveillance practices of the NSA?

"I want to spark a worldwide debate about privacy, Internet freedom, and the dangers of state surveillance," he stated. "I'm not afraid of what will happen to me. I've accepted that my life will be over from my doing this. I'm at peace with that. I know it's the right thing to do."

The next step was for Glenn and Laura to travel to Hong Kong to meet the whistleblower – Edward Snowden, a 29-year-old who had worked since 2005 as a technical expert for the CIA, NSA and its sub-contractors, making around $200,000 in salary and bonuses. He had travelled to Hong Kong in May, staying in a hotel under his own name, figuring he was safer there than staying in the US when news of the leaked documents broke.

"I watched NSA tracking people's Internet activities as they typed. I became aware of just how invasive US surveillance capabilities had become. I realised the true breadth of this system. And almost nobody knew it was happening."

"For many kids, the Internet is a means of self-actualisation. It allows them to explore who they are and who they want to be, but that works only if we're able to be private and anonymous, to make mistakes without them following us. I worry that mine will be the last generation to enjoy that freedom. I do not want to live in a world where we have no privacy and no freedom, where the unique value of the Internet is snuffed out."

On 6th June 2013, the first of many articles was published by the Guardian.

NSA collecting phone records of millions of Verizon customers daily

Exclusive: Top secret court order requiring Verizon to hand over all call data shows scale of domestic surveillance under President Obama.

The order, signed by Judge Roger Vinson, compels Verizon to produce to the NSA electronic copies of "all call detail records or 'telephony metadata' created by Verizon for communications between the United States and abroad" or "wholly within the United States, including local telephone calls".

As journalist Glenn Greenwald painstakingly sifted through the mountain of information provided by Snowden, he was shocked at the extent of the American surveillance operation. It included the NSA's tapping of Internet servers, satellites, underwater fibre-optic cables, local and foreign telephone systems and personal computers. A list of individuals targeted for particularly invasive forms of spying included suspected terrorist and criminal suspects, democratically elected leaders of many countries in Europe including France and Germany, and ordinary American citizens.

6-35

The documents leaked by Snowden revealed that the literal aim of the US Government was to collect, store, monitor and analyse metadata (for example, number called, date, time and duration of call) about all electronic communications by everybody in the world. In one month in 2013, the unit collected data on more than 97 billion emails and 124 billion phone calls from around the world.

Case study 2: Cyber-attacks

Estonia suffers a cyber-attack

Way back in 2007, Estonia suffered a series of cyber-attacks which swamped websites of organisations including The Estonian Parliament, banks, ministries, newspapers and broadcasters. This was one of the largest cases of state-sponsored cyber warfare ever seen, sponsored by Russia in retaliation for the relocation of the Bronze Soldier of Tallinn, an elaborate Soviet-era grave marker, and war graves in Tallinn.

In 2008, an ethnic Russian Estonian national was charged and convicted of the crime.

Sony Pictures is hacked

Sony's film *The Interview*, is an action comedy film in which two journalists are instructed to assassinate North Korean leader Kim Jong-un, and in which the leader is shown in an unflattering light. In June 2014, the North Korean government threatened merciless action against the United States if the film's distributor released the film. Columbia delayed the release from October to December, editing it to make it more acceptable to North Korea. However, in November, Sony Pictures computers were hacked by the "Guardians of Peace", a group the FBI believes was linked to the North Korean Government. Several other forthcoming films and other sensitive information was leaked, and threats of terrorist attacks against cinemas which showed the film were threatened.

Case study 3: Google Street View

Google Street View was integrated into Google Earth in 2008. It provides panoramic street-level views and users can view selected streets in villages, towns and cities in hundreds of countries in every continent throughout the world, including 99% of UK streets. Photos previously taken by a camera mounted on an automobile are stored with the software and users can view the street from any direction and at a variety of angles.

The photos, featuring passers-by without their consent as well as the cars on the street, are freely available to anyone, worldwide. What are the ethical issues involved here? Does the 'principle of informed consent' apply? Google Street View brings convenience to people's lives, but some would say it is a dangerous invasion of privacy. On the one hand, it enables people to check out places they are intending to visit, such as the location of a hotel or a friend's house. On the other hand, it could enable criminals to 'case the joint' that they are intending to burgle, from the privacy of their own home, determine the location of security cameras, locate utility boxes for power or gas, and check out the types of gates, doors and windows.

Google has taken some measures to protect privacy. People's faces and car number plates are blurred out, and individuals and organisations can request that certain images be blurred or removed. However, in some instances, individuals can still be recognisable even with pixelated faces.

> **Q1:** Imagine you are a Google Project Manager and have been asked to evaluate a proposal to bring Google Street View technology to a remote African village. What questions should be asked? Who should be consulted? What benefits, risks and safeguards should be considered?

Exercises

1. Do you think Edward Snowden was right to reveal the secret documents to which he had access, being legally forbidden to do so under the US Espionage Act 1917? Justify your answer. [4]

2. The FBI and NSA have been protesting about losing surveillance capabilities—through greater encryption of the Internet—since the 1990s. In China, the manufacture, use, sale, import, or export of any item containing encryption without prior government approval may lead to administrative fines, the seizure of equipment, confiscation of illegal gains, and even criminal prosecution.

    Give arguments for and against a policy of making it illegal for individuals and organisations to use strong encryption in their online communications. [4]

3. Among the papers exposed by Edward Snowden was President Barack Obama's presidential directive to prepare offensive cyber-operations.

    Describe some of the possible reasons for this directive. [4]

6-35

Chapter 36 – The challenges of the digital age

Objectives

- Discuss how developments in computer science have enabled massive transformations in the capacity to distribute, publish, communicate and disseminate personal information

- Understand that software and their algorithms embed moral and cultural values

- Understand the real and potential impact that digital technology has on employment, the distribution of wealth and the lives of millions of people

The economic impact of the Internet

The Internet has its origins in the 1960s with ARPANET, the first North American wide area network. In 1974, two engineers called Bob Kahn and Vint Cerf devised a protocol for linking up individual networks into what they termed the Internet – the "internetworking of networks".

In the 1980s Tim Berners-Lee, working for CERN in Geneva, invented, or designed, the World Wide Web. He wrote his initial Web proposal in March 1989 and in 1990 built the first Web browser, called WorldWideWeb. His vision was that "all the bits of information in every computer in CERN, and on the planet, would be available to me and to anyone else. There would be a single global information space."

Berners-Lee had little interest in money and gave away his technology for nothing, but one of the most significant consequences of his invention was a complete reshaping of the economy throughout the world. Has it created jobs, or simply created the "1% economy" in which the top Internet companies like Google, Amazon, Facebook, Instagram and others have accumulated huge wealth at the expense of thousands of workers?

6-36

Amazon

Amazon started as an online bookstore in 1994 but soon diversified into DVDs, software, video games, toys, furniture, clothes and thousands of other products. In 2013 the company turned over $75 billion in sales. It now accounts for 65% of all digital purchases of book sales, but in Britain, for example, there are now fewer than 4,000 bookstores, one third less than in 2005. Where a bookshop employs 47 people for every $10 million in sales, Amazon employs 14 to generate the same revenue.

eBay

eBay, essentially an electronic platform bringing together buyers and sellers of goods, grew from a user base of 41,000 trading goods worth $7.2 million in 1995, to 162 million users trading goods worth $227.9 billion in 2014.

Google

In 1996, Larry Page and Sergey Brin, two Stanford University Computer Science postgraduate students, created Google. There were already several successful search engines like Yahoo and AltaVista on the market, but Page and Brin came up with a game-changing algorithm, which they called PageRank, for determining the relevance of a Web page based on the number and quality of its incoming links. The idea was that you could estimate the importance of a Web page by the number and status of other web pages that link to it. Every time you make a search, the Google search engine becomes more knowledgeable and thus more useful. Even more valuable to Google is the fact that Google learns more about you every time you search.

By 1998, Google was getting 10,000 queries every day. By 1999, they were getting 70 million daily requests. Their next step was to figure out how to make money out of their free technology, and they came up with AdWords, which enabled advertisers to place keyword-associated ads down the right hand side of the page. The image below shows what comes up when a user in Dorchester searches for "Paintball", with the nearest companies, sponsored advertisements and a map with their locations.

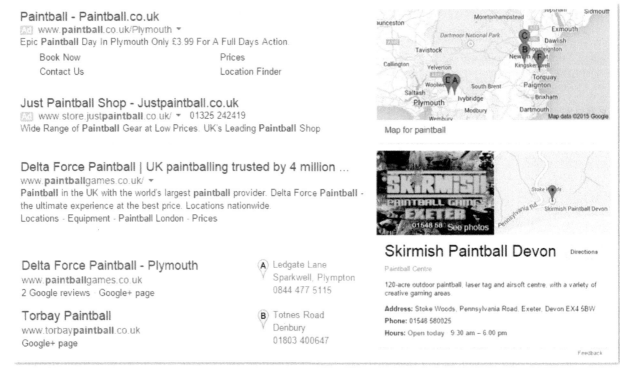

By 2014, Google had joined Amazon as a winner-takes-all company, with 1.5 billion daily searches and revenues of $50 billion.

The destruction of jobs

A 2013 paper by Carl Benedikt Frey and Michael Osborne entitled *"The Future of Employment: how susceptible are jobs to computerisation?"* estimates that 47% of total US employment is at risk. They examine the impact of future computerisation on more than 700 individual occupations, and note the shifting of labour from middle-income manufacturing jobs to low-income service jobs which are less susceptible to computerisation. At the same time, with falling prices of computing, problem-solving skills are becoming relatively productive, explaining the substantial employment growth in occupations involving cognitive tasks where skilled, well-educated labour has a comparative advantage.

The disappearance of middle-income occupations has caused a polarization of labour, with growing employment in high-income cognitive jobs and low-income manual labour. Driverless cars developed by Google are an example of how computerisation is no longer confined to routine manufacturing tasks. The possibility of drones delivering your parcels is no longer in the realms of science fiction. In the 10 jobs that have a 99% likelihood of being replaced by software and automation within the next 25 years, Frey and Osbourne include tax preparers, library assistants, clothing factory workers, and photographic process workers.

In fact, jobs in the photographic industry have already all but vanished. In 1989, when Tim Berners-Lee invented the Internet, Kodak employed 145,000 people in research labs, offices and factories in Rochester US and had a market value of $31 billion. In 2013 the company filed for bankruptcy and Rochester became virtually a ghost town.

Meanwhile, in 2010, a young entrepreneur called Kevin Systrom started up Instagram, which enabled users to create photos on their smartphones with filters to give them, for example, a warm and fuzzy glow.

An Instagram moment

Twenty-five thousand iPhone users downloaded the app when it launched on 6th October 2010. A month later, Systrom's Instagram had a million members. By early 2012, it had 14 million users and by November, 100 million users, with the app hosting 5 billion photos. When Systrom sold Instagram to Facebook for a billion dollars in 2012 (less than two years after the startup), Instagram still only had thirteen full-time employees working out of a small office in San Fransisco. It is a good example of a service that is not providing any jobs at all in the winner-takes-all economics of the digital marketplace.

6-36

User-generated content

In his book "The Cult of the Amateur", Andrew Keen argues that *"MySpace and Facebook are creating a youth culture of digital narcissism; open-source knowledge-sharing sites like Wikipedia are undermining the authority of teachers in the classroom, the YouTube generation are more interested in self-expression than in learning about the outside world; the cacophony of anonymous blogs and user-generated content is deafening today's user to the voices of informed experts and professional journalism; kids are so busy self-broadcasting themselves on social networks that they no longer consume the creative work of professional musicians, novelists, or filmmakers."*

Keen asserts that a thriving music, video and publishing economy is being replaced by the multi-billion dollar monopolist YouTube. The traditional copyright-intensive industries accounted for almost 510 billion Euros in the European Union during the period 2008-2010, and generated 3.2% of all jobs, amounting to more than 7 million jobs. What will happen if large numbers of these jobs disappear?

Trolls on the Internet

Trolls, cyber-bullying and misogyny have become a fact of everyday life on the Internet. It wasn't supposed to be this way – the Internet was going to inspire a generation to voice a broad diversity of opinion and empower those who traditionally had no voice.

After the 2010-11 Arab Spring, many people argued that the social media networks were helping to overthrow dictatorships and empower the people. But the Arab Spring deteriorated into vicious religious and ethnic civil wars, culminating in the rise of the so-called ISIS, which uses social networks to post atrocities and radicalise young Muslims.

Feminist writers and journalists, academics like Mary Beard and political campaigner Caroline Criado-Perez, who petitioned the Bank of England to create a bank note featuring a woman's face, receive hundreds of death threats and rape threats for no other reason than that they are women who have dared to appear on the media. Thousands of other women and teenage girls are victims of similar trolling on the Internet. Savage bullying on various social networking sites has led to several tragic cases of suicide.

The Internet has brought great benefits, but all of us have a responsibility to use it wisely and well.

Algorithms and ethics

Computer scientists and software engineers who devise the multitude of algorithms used by YouTube, Facebook, Amazon and Google, and by organisations from banks and Stock Exchanges to the Health Service and the police, have significant power and therefore the responsibility that goes with it. In some US cities, algorithms determine whether you are likely to be stopped and searched on the street. Banks use algorithms to decide whether to consider your application for a mortgage or a loan. Algorithms are applied to decision-making in hiring and firing, healthcare and advertising. It has been reported, for example, that some algorithms which decide what advertisements are shown on your browser screen classify web users into categories which include "probably bipolar", "daughter killed in car crash", "rape victim", and "gullible elderly".[i] Did the programmer who wrote that algorithm have any qualms about his work?

When algorithms prioritise, they "bring attention to certain things at the expense of others".[ii] Facebook's 'News Feed' product filters posts, stories and activities undertaken by friends. Content for the Newsfeed is selected or omitted according to a ranking algorithm which Facebook, with its billion-plus user base, continually develops and tests to show users the content they will be most interested in. But it has been suggested that these social interactions may influence people's emotions and state of mind; the emotions expressed by friends via online social networks may influence our own moods and behaviour.[iii] Clearly, then, those who devise the ranking algorithms potentially have the ability to influence the emotional state of people using Facebook.

Should computer scientists consider the institutional goals of a prospective employer, or the social worth of what they do, before accepting a job? Phillip Rogway, Professor of Computer Science at the University of California, found that on a Google search of deciding among job offers, not one suggested that this was a factor. [iv]

The Internet of things

As digital technologies are used in more and more areas of our lives, spreading into our offline environments through the so-called 'Internet of things', previously inert objects are expected to become networked and start making decisions for us. Algorithms will allow the refrigerator to decide what food needs replacing, a door will decide who to let in. Should your door call the police if the door is opened by someone without a tracking device? Should your house report a child, who screams excessively, to the Social Services?

Driverless cars

The prospect of large numbers of self-driving cars on our roads raises ethical questions about the morality of different algorithms which could be used in the face of causing "unavoidable harm" - who gets harmed and who gets spared. [v]

(a) The car can stay on course and kill several pedestrians, or swerve and kill one passer-by

(b) The car can stay on course and kill one pedestrian, or swerve and kill its passenger

(c) The car can stay on course and kill several pedestrians, or swerve and kill its passenger

The MIT Technology Review asked: "Should different decisions be made when children are on board, since they both have a longer time ahead of them than adults, and had less say in being in the car in the first place? If a manufacturer offers different versions of its moral algorithm, and a buyer knowingly chose one of them, is the buyer to blame for the harmful consequences of the algorithm's decisions?"

One of the commonly held principles that form a commonly held set of pillars for moral life is the obligation not to inflict harm intentionally; in medical ethics, the physician's guiding principle is "Do no harm". Going further, the moral duties of all scientists, including computer scientists, should also include trying to promote the common good.

(i)   *Naughton, John, The Guardian (2015, December 6) "Algorithm writers need a code of conduct" www.theguardian.com/commentisfree/2015/dec/06/algorithm-writers-should-have-code-of-conduct*

(ii) *Centre of Internet & Human Rights (2015) "The ethics of Algorithms: from radical content to self-driving cars". Retrieved from www.gccs2015.com/sites/default/files/documents/ Ethics_Algorithms-final%20doc.pdf*

(iii) *Kramer, Adam et al (2014, March 25) "Experimental evidence of massive-scale emotional contagion through social networks". Retrieved from http://www.pnas.org/content/111/24/8788.full*

(iv) *Rogway, Phillip (2015, December 12) "The Moral Character of Cryptographic Work". Retrieved from http://web.cs.ucdavis.edu/~rogaway/papers/moral-fn.pdf*

(v)   *Owano, Nancy (2015 October 24) "When self-driving cars drive the ethical questions". Retrieved from http://techxplore.com/news/2015-10-self-driving-cars-ethical.html*

6-36

Challenges facing legislators in the digital age

Legislation relating to privacy can be broadly categorised into laws intended to protect personal privacy and those which have been passed in the interests of national security, crime detection or counter-terrorism.

Some laws relate specifically to computing, for example:

* the Data Protection Act (1998) which is designed to ensure that personal data is kept accurate, up-to-date, safe and secure and not used in ways which would harm individuals.

* the Computer Misuse Act, which makes it an offence to access computer material without permission, or to modify it without permission.

Other laws such as the Copyright, Designs and Patents Act (1988) have a more general application, covering the intellectual property rights of many types of work including books, music, art, computer programs and other original works.

The rapidly changing field of computing and worldwide communications poses particular challenges to legislators.

- Countries have different laws, and it is sometimes hard to prove in which country an offence was committed, and equally hard to trace the offender or to prosecute.

- New applications in Computing are constantly being invented and with them, new ways of committing offences for which there is no legislation.

Legislators have to balance the rights of the individual with the need for security and protection from terrorist or criminal activity. Many countries, for example, have enacted legislation restricting or banning the use of strong cryptography.

> **Q1:** How concerned are you about misuse of your personal data? Are you aware of how your social profile may be used by future employers?
>
> Find some examples of the application of the Computer Misuse Act
> (e.g. www.computerevidence.co.uk/Cases/CMA.htm)

Exercises

1. Networking sites frequently feature angry, violent or inaccurate content.

   Should Facebook, Twitter, Ask.com and others take responsibility for content posted on their sites? What sort of content should not be allowed? Would it be possible to develop software to facilitate such a task? Discuss. [5]

2. Some of the jobs likely to disappear over the next decade owing to computerisation include manufacturing jobs, clerical jobs and even service jobs, where people will be replaced by robots. Give examples of other jobs which may be lost owing to computerisation. What will be the social effects of the job losses? [5]

3. In September 2015, the Environmental Protection Agency (EPA) found that many VW cars being sold in America had a "defeat device" embedded in the software that could detect when diesel engines were being tested, changing the performance accordingly to improve results. The German car giant has since admitted cheating emissions tests in the US. In October 2015, the company posted its first loss for 15 years, of 2.5 billion euros. In 2016 VW will recall millions of cars and in addition to the cost of doing this, could face fines from the EPA of up to $18 billion.

   Research this case and find answers to some the questions this case raises. For example:

   - Who is responsible for wilfully using "defeat devices" in the software used in the emissions tests?
   - What was the motivation of the perpetrators?
   - Who in the company is ultimately responsible for this situation?
   - Do you consider that the software engineers involved "caused great harm"? If so, in what way?

4. Decisions are often made about us on the basis of algorithms of which we may be completely unaware.

   Car insurance premiums are calculated based largely on your age, experience, address, occupation and vehicle details. Health insurance premiums are affected by age, occupation, personal and parental medical histories. Are the algorithms that calculate these premiums fair? Discuss how the algorithms used embed moral and/or cultural values. State with reasons who benefits from the decisions made by these algorithms and whether anyone is harmed. [4]

6-36

References

The following books have been useful in writing this book and will provide interesting and illuminating background reading for this course, for both teachers and students.

Beecher, Karl, "Brown dogs and barbers – What's Computer Science all about?", 2014

Greenwald, Glen, "No Place to Hide: Edward Snowden, the NSA and the Surveillance State", McLelland and Stewart, 2014

Harding, Luke, "The Snowden files: The Inside Story of the World's Most Wanted Man", Vintage Books, 2014

Hey, Tony and Pápay, Gyuri, "The Computing Universe", Cambridge University Press, 2015

Keen, Andrew, "The Cult of the Amateur", Nicholas Brealey Publishing, 2007, 2008

Keen, Andrew, "The Internet is not the Answer", Atlantic Books, London, 2015

Levitin, Anany and Levitin, Maria, "Algorithmic puzzles", Oxford University Press, 2011

Index

Index

Index

Lightning Source UK Ltd.
Milton Keynes UK
UKOW07f0845130916

282805UK00009B/53/P

9 781910 523063